SEVEN CENTURIES
OF WESTERN ART

Giotto di Bondone, father of Italian Renaissance painting, was born in 1266. José Clemente Orozco, great Mexican muralist, the last artist represented in this book, died in 1949.

In the centuries between, all the great schools of Western Art rose and flourished, from Leonardo and Michelangelo in Italy; El Greco, Velásquez and Goya in Spain; Rubens, Vermeer and Rembrandt in the Low Countries; Poussin, Watteau and Chardin in France; Gainsborough, Constable, Turner in England; the French precursors of the Impressionists, Delacroix, Daumier, Courbet; Cézanne, Manet, Degas; the Impressionists who changed the face of modern art; Picasso and the Cubists; Kokoschka and the German Expressionists, to Kandinsky and the present-day abstractionists.

In text and illustrations, 50 GREAT ARTISTS provides a succinct history of these seven centuries of Western Art.

BANTAM MATRIX EDITIONS

fifty
great artists

·

by Bernard Myers

·

BANTAM BOOKS
NEW YORK/TORONTO/LONDON

FIFTY GREAT ARTISTS

A Bantam Book / published December 1953
2nd printing....September 1957
Bantam Classic edition published October 1959
4th printing.........July 1962
5th printing......February 1963
Bantam Matrix edition published November 1965
7th printing.........July 1966
8th printing.........July 1967

Library of Congress Catalog Card Number: 65-26641

Bantam Books are published by Bantam Books, Inc., a subsidiary
of Grosset & Dunlap, Inc. Its trade-mark, consisting of the words
"Bantam Books" and the portrayal of a bantam, is registered in the
United States Patent Office and in other countries. Marca Registrada.
Bantam Books, Inc., 271 Madison Avenue, New York, N.Y. 10016.

PRINTED IN THE UNITED STATES OF AMERICA

FOR MY SON PETER

ACKNOWLEDGMENTS

The author wishes to thank the museums and collectors whose generosity has made possible the inclusion of many items reproduced in this volume. Special thanks are due the National Gallery in Washington, D.C., through whose kindness the color plates were made available.

CONTENTS

LIST OF ILLUSTRATIONS

The color plates for 50 GREAT ARTISTS were made available by the National Gallery of Art, Washington, D. C. The production of these unusually fine color plates begins with a highly experienced photographer who supplies separation negatives made directly from the paintings. From these negatives one of the country's foremost engravers, the Beck Engraving Company, etches plates which are then proved, corrected, and compared with the original paintings, until the closest possible fidelity to color and value is obtained.

FOREWORD

Millions of Americans in all parts of the country provide an audience for national radio, television, magazine and newspaper offerings in the field of art. These same millions are responsible for the growing attendance figures at museums, the increased sale of art books, magazines and color prints, the dozens of schools and adult courses, the sponsorship of art centers.

Thanks to public education and the various kinds of mass communication, we have become the most culture-conscious nation on earth. Today there are more people taking part in art, music, theater, dance, literary and other cultural activities than ever before in history. Although we may not be producing masterpieces in the old sense or even enjoying the same high level of individual appreciation on which the Old World flatters itself, we do have a wider degree of interest in the arts than any other population can boast at the moment. This is another form of our democracy.

This awareness of art has been one of the last to establish itself; it has all happened within the past fifteen years. Today the man in the street and the student both turn to it as formerly they did only to music and books. For them, art may express pure physical beauty or appeal to the emotions, it may be an intellectual experience in which one element balances another, or it may have symbolic ideas with far-reaching and even universal meaning. All these things can be found in music and literature. It is art alone, however, that shows them in a visual form. We can actually see the way that people lived and thought, the clothes they wore, how they loved, worshipped, fought and died. And here, above all, is visibly recorded the growth of the human spirit.

This book is a response to the nation-wide trend, with certain special advantages. Through the mass production methods of paper-back books, this short history offers close to a hundred black and white illustrations and sixteen color plates as well as a book-length text giving a concise story of the development of Western painting up to the present day. Finally there is a consistent attempt to relate the various painters in this pocket-size museum to the times in which they lived. For although each artist is a personality unto himself, he is also a product of the time in which he lived.

The purpose has been to explain why the fifty masters chosen here are important, how they express their times in history, how they compare with their contemporaries, what they have contributed to the craft of painting and to the enrichment of the human spirit.

The artists have been divided according to period. First comes the era of change from the Middle Ages to the early Renaissance (fourteenth and fifteenth centuries), then the Renaissance proper and the Mannerist period following it (sixteenth century). After these are the Baroque masters of the seventeenth century and the Rococo and middle class painters of the eighteenth century. Finally we have the artists of the turbulent nineteenth century and the painters of our own day from Cézanne to Beckmann and Orozco.

Our story of the growth of Western painting is really the story of the birth of modern man. A thousand or so years separate the fall of ancient civilization and the beginning of the modern world. During these years the well-organized empire of the Romans fell apart. Tribes of northern barbarians warred on one another, sacked the cities and allowed the roads and aqueducts to crumble into ruins. For centuries, the Western world fell into isolated communities —small, self-sustaining islands frozen by rigid caste systems in which every man knew his place from birth. Gradually, however, new forms of social organization did develop. With the beginning of the Crusades the old trade routes were re-established. Towns and cities grew up and freemen and escaped serfs became merchants, bankers or guildsmen. In the freer atmosphere of the towns, man began to investigate the nature of the world about him. We begin our story with the fourteenth century because at that point the results of the new individualism and the new search for truth reached their first climax. In that period the individual human being became someone to be cherished; portraits were painted, biographies written, and a literature and an art were developed which, for the first time since the fall of Rome, focused on everyday, living people instead of on religion alone.

Town life developed most quickly in Italy. A favorable location across the path of the Crusades enabled the Italian merchants to make an enormous amount of money in supplying and financing the various expeditions from northern Europe to the Holy Land. Moreover, Italy had never been as deeply involved in the rigidity of feudal life, and so the competitive element could flourish here before it came into being elsewhere. This not only developed business individualism; it also brought into being a sense of free enterprise in all areas, an investigating spirit in art, science, and politics that characterizes the entire period which we call the Renaissance.

It is true, of course, that the Renaissance marks a period of learning, but this does not mean that earlier periods were ignorant. What is significant is that the learning of the fourteenth to sixteenth centuries took a new direction— toward a new-found human dignity modeled on that of the

ancient world, and toward the idea of finding out, questioning, discovering.

The Renaissance is often called the Age of Discovery.
Leonardo da Vinci and others studied the human body,
geological and botanical structure, the nature of mechanics
and many other scientific phenomena. It is also the age in
which the New World was explored by Columbus, Amerigo
Vespucci, Magellan, and many others. In all these ex-
plorations and discoveries the keynote was individuality,
but it is in art that this spirit first showed itself. During this
period the arts were perhaps more important than they
have ever been since, because in them were mirrored the
new probing for truth, the concentration on man, and the
rediscovery of the Greek and Roman classics. Even more
significant is the fact that art was the real and only store-
house of science in an age when science as such did not yet
exist.

Like any other productive worker, the Renaissance artist
himself was a respectable member of society—the maker of
a product for which there was a real demand. His place in
society was not only assured; with men like Raphael, Titian,
Michelangelo and Jan van Eyck, it was extremely high. In
fifteenth century Italy a man was as good as his good right
arm or his sensitive eye; there was no limit to what could
be accomplished. With the late sixteenth and seventeenth
centuries and the growth of centralized monarchies, the
position of the artist became less secure. More and more he
came to depend on a royal, somewhat personal, and often
capricious patronage. As the artists guilds of an earlier period disappeared their place was taken by governmentally
regulated academies. The artist had either to conform or to
find a market among the rising middle class. This is the
crisis of the late seventeenth and eighteenth centuries. The
events of the French Revolution cast the artist adrift once
and for all on the stream of free competition. Like all men
he had to sell his products or his skill where he could. From
this circumstance, perhaps, come many problems of the
twentieth-century painter—his feeling of dislocation, his

belief that he has no truly understanding audience. Although, as a result, the artist may take refuge in a highly personal, even obscure kind of art, his work is still a genuine expression of the times in which we live.

BERNARD MYERS

GIOTTO DI BONDONE

Our story of painting in the Western world begins with the thirteenth-century pioneer Giotto. From the relatively stiff artistic background of his time, he developed a majestic, sculptural style which set Italian art on its future path. Although his technical contribution to painting is enormous, Giotto's great feeling for humanity makes his work a high point in the movement toward the humanizing of art and life begun early in the century. In both respects he is a key figure, his personality stamped on the whole course of Italian art. For more than two hundred years after his death artists acknowledged their debt to this master of monumental dignity and controlled emotional strength.

Son of a peasant who had apparently acquired some land and stock of his own, Giotto was early apprenticed to the Florentine painter Cimabue. According to the legend, the boy first attracted attention with sketches of his father's sheep drawn on slate with sharp stone. Impressed, Cimabue took him to Assisi. There the young Giotto helped with the frescoes (wall paintings on fresh plaster) in the great church of St. Francis. This center of the growing Franciscan movement had become the crossroads of Italian art. Here the young apprentice absorbed both the flat-patterned, emotional art of his own teacher and the rounded forms of the painters from Rome who had been influenced by the ancient sculptures in the Eternal City. Giotto combined these qualities to form a new and personal style.

Later, after a few years as director of the Assisi project,

Giotto was called to Rome to help celebrate the jubilee of 1300. There he completed a mosaic of Christ saving St. Peter from the waves which still may be seen, though in a restored and transformed state. In this work the art of ancient Rome again influenced him toward the powerful three-dimensional forms of sculpture.

A number of years later Giotto was called to Padua by the wealthy Enrico Scrovegni who had built the Arena Chapel in honor of the Virgin Annunciate and to help the repose of his father's soul. The necessity of this gesture may be judged by the fact that this notorious moneylender is found in the seventh circle of Dante's Hell. Dividing the side walls of the simple brick structure into three rows, Giotto painted scenes from the life of the Virgin and Christ. A Last Judgment on the whole of the entrance wall shows Scrovegni himself presenting the chapel to three angels. Easily the greatest of his undisputed works, Giotto has here projected one of the most impressive series of pictures in all Christian art. Powerful but gracious figures move about serenely, their white robes touched with grayish green, blue or pink. It is as though the great sculptures of the cathedrals of the Middle Ages had come to life and moved out of their niches into the world of men.

One of the frescoes shows *Joachim and Anna* (fig. 1), the parents of the Virgin, meeting at the Beautiful Gate. These sad and childless middle aged people had been living apart, she at home and he in the fields with his flocks. When they both had visions foretelling the birth of a child, they left house and flocks and rushed to see each other.

No romantic youngsters, these are staid older people greeting each other with great warmth, but without frenzy —their feelings mirrored in the faces of the women at the right. Joachim puts his hands gently on Anna's shoulders and as he raises his arms the cloth tightens about his back, giving form and solidity to his figure.

Two things are especially noteworthy in the Arena Chapel frescoes. First, the tangible sense of form conveyed by the force and direction of the powerful outlines. These

1 GIOTTO *The Meeting of Joachim and Anna*

suggest bulk beneath the clothes, the actual feeling of a body with solid existence. Second, the artist injects a special quality of dignity and restraint that balances the dramatic tension of the stories. This element, perhaps derived from the relatively unemotional art of antiquity, leaves the actors under the artist's control.

Giotto's artistic intent may be compared with that of his great countryman, the epic poet Dante. Both Florentines, they were interested in the projection of profound but restrained human dramas, stories in which human sorrows and passions are examined with the greatest sympathy and with an equally great sense of decorum. We know that Dante visited Giotto during the Paduan project where he is supposed to have jokingly remarked on the difference between the ugly faces of the painter's children and the idealized faces in the frescoes. Giotto replied that the portraits of the saints, unlike the less favored children, had been created when there was plenty of light to work by.

In a second St. Francis cycle done for the church of Santa Croce in Florence, Giotto repeated the powerful sculpturesque impressions and sense of dignity achieved at Padua. To these elements he added the quality of decorative symmetry. The *Death of St. Francis* (fig. 2) reveals a carefully balanced composition which increases the effectiveness of the presentation in a way that was to become increasingly characteristic of Italian art.

In a neat shallow box space the deathbed is flanked by two doorways, each with its group of five mourners. Another five stand against the rear wall, while three figures kneel on either side of the bed. The actuality and solidity of these figures is heightened by the draperies covering them. This powerful impression of form is apparent even over the shoes of the foreground characters whose faces are not seen but whose reality cannot be doubted.

Everything in the position and glances of the mourners draws us to the dying saint, giving not merely a succession of details but a totality of immediate impact. Only one person, the monk visible above St. Francis' halo, is diverted

2   GIOTTO   *Death of St. Francis*

Santa Croce, Florence (Anderson)

from this complete unity. As though to remind us of the divine nature of this moment his eyes are drawn to the vision of the saint's soul moving heavenward. However human their emotions of sorrow, these are superhuman beings, moving about in an ideal rather than everyday form—in the eloquently dignified manner that identifies the new style begun by Giotto.

MASACCIO

(*Tomaso Guidi*)

ALTHOUGH Masaccio died at the age of twenty-seven, his personality made a tremendous impression on Italian painting. For generations afterward painters marveled at his frescoes in the Brancacci Chapel of the Carmine Church in Florence, wondering how he achieved his new lighting, his spatial and atmospheric effects. To this unofficial academy painters like Leonardo, Raphael, and Michelangelo came to study and work..

Giotto's method had been to outline the figure and, through the powerful contour, suggest a third dimension. Line was a shorthand method of indicating form; it carried the eye of the spectator in the directions desired by the painter. Masaccio's method is illustrated by the famous *The Tribute Money* (fig. 3) of the Brancacci Chapel. It differentiates between the light that falls on a rounded figure and the shadows it casts—more or less what actually happens in nature. The light-and-dark, or *chiaroscuro*, technique was conceived almost at one stroke. During a period of perhaps three years the artist developed this new way of building up the mass of a form and of placing it in a given part of a three-dimensional space. The effect of his remarkable feat can be traced in the work of the great masters of the High Renaissance.

Masaccio was also able to portray figures out of doors so convincingly that they appear to blur as they move away from us. Linear perspective reproduces the effect of forms growing smaller in the distance. With his new aerial perspective Masaccio pointed out that they also grow dimmer and out of focus.

About the Christ in *The Tribute Money* are massed the twelve disciples and the Roman tax gatherer demanding his poll tax. Between the figures a tangible sensation of air has been inserted. It extends out among the trees and hills and into the atmosphere beyond. A solid massive feeling of sculptural roundness is achieved with the new chiaroscuro technique. The apparent weight of the light-modeled figures makes their feet seem to cling to the ground. Another major step has been taken along the path originally laid out by Giotto.

Most important, perhaps, is the sense of dignity conferred on these persons. A respect for the individual is a basic part of the Renaissance and reflects the liberation of man from medieval anonymity. Masaccio's religious parable —the story of Peter's violent refusal to pay the Roman tax collector—does not neglect the human for the spiritual. The scenes show Christ's majestic gesture leading His angry disciple to a stream to catch a fish from which a coin is extracted. As Peter still rebels against paying the tribute, he is asked "Whose head is on this coin, Peter?" When the latter answers, "Caesar's, Lord," he is told "Render unto Caesar what is Caesar's and unto God what is God's."

And so in the third episode of this continuous narration Peter, framed in the archway at the right, turns the coin over to the hawk-faced official.

The handsome and dignified Christ became a standard for painters during the succeeding centuries. Each of the other carefully differentiated faces has its own personality. The character at the extreme right is supposed to be the painter himself.

One of the dominant characteristics of the figures of Masaccio is the general rather than specific way in which they are painted. Instead of a photographic and detailed image, a large, massive, undetailed impression of form gives

3 MASACCIO *The Tribute Money*

Church of the Carmine, Florence (Anderson)

the feeling of three dimensions. This may be seen in *The Tribute Money* and in *The Expulsion from Paradise* (fig. 4), another panel from the same chapel.

In the latter, Adam and Eve are driven from the gateway of Eden into the world beyond by the quiet, relentless angel hovering overhead. The angel's outspread arms provide a frame which helps keep the composition together. Unity is also tightened through the parallel arrangement of the two pairs of legs. A gradation of light to dark moves from the right to the left side on each of the human forms. Just as the figures are broad indications of the mass rather than a heaping up of little details, the emotions portrayed are more symbolic than actual. These emotions represent not merely the shame of Adam and Eve, but the reactions of humankind. Thus Adam covers his face in genuine remorse while Eve, though ashamed enough, is inclined to take this as a kind of personal affront, crying and wailing as she goes on into the future.

In spite of the strength of feeling, the emotions never get out of hand. There is always a good measure of restraint, a balance of dramatic power and artistic control typical of the movement as a whole. This, and the generalization of form with its monumental quality, is what is meant by the classical feeling of these pictures. In them as in the paintings of Giotto and later in those of Leonardo, Raphael, and Michelangelo, the impact of the work is immediate and concentrated. The eye is drawn at once to the central and important part. Without hesitation the spectator is brought to the heart of an epic but human situation.

4

MASACCIO

*The
Expulsion
from
Paradise*

*Church of the
Carmine, Florence
(Anderson)*

PIERO DELLA FRANCESCA

THE Renaissance was an age of intellectual exploration—architects, sculptors, and painters investigated the nature of the world around them and contributed many significant ideas to the sum total of human knowledge. These men who studied mathematics, anatomy, and other disciplines in the interest of their art were the true scientists of their day. Contemporary historians recorded this twofold achievement. To his age Piero della Francesca was not only a leading painter, he was recognized as its greatest geometrician as well.

Although Piero had been an apprentice in Florence, the cultural center of fifteenth-century Italy, he lived most of his life in the quiet provinces. Yet he reflects the great investigating urge of the time, the feeling that one should find out what makes things work. In his search for new technical methods, his stressing of controlled power and impressive sculpturesque forms, Piero is part of the Florentine movement begun by Giotto and Masaccio. At the age of sixty he abandoned painting and retired to his native town. There he wrote a rather complicated and unreadable book on perspective, studied anatomy and proportion, and wrote a second book on the five regular solids. It was his intention to provide a sound mathematical foundation for future generations of artists.

The most striking artistic contributions made by Piero are an extension of the atmospheric techniques by Masaccio and a deliberate freezing of his monumental forms. The

5   PIERO DELLA FRANCESCA   *The Nativity*

6 PIERO DELLA FRANCESCA *The Resurrection of Ch*

well-known *The Nativity* (fig. 5) also shows the first attempt to portray real sunlight: the light that falls on the top of the rude shelter. This light describes a specific time of day; it cuts diagonally across the picture, leaving the Madonna's face partly in shadow and the faces of the three shepherds at the right completely shadowed. Beyond this primary illumination, the painter makes the light lead us deeper and deeper into the picture space. Objects in the foreground are seen crisply, sharply, and in dark tones, those in the middleground are colored more lightly, and those in the background are lightest of all. The general color tonality of such pictures is purposely limited to silvery grays in an all-over effect that resembles modern Impressionist outdoor painting.

The remarkable series of frescoes finished in 1466, depicting *The Story of the True Cross*, is on a somewhat different and much more austere level. This is Piero's most ambitious project and is comparable in importance with the earlier Masaccio and Giotto commissions.

The seriousness of these frescoes is repeated by Piero's wall painting, the famous *The Resurrection of Christ* (fig. 6), in the Palazzo Comunale of his home town Borgo San Sepolcro. This representation of the Patron and Protector of the city, the Resurrected Christ, is in many ways one of the most effective of Piero's compositions. The figures are close to the main line of the picture, arranged like a pyramid against the deep landscape with a mysterious early morning sky and fleecy clouds. Here Christ, stark and immobile, rises from another world to confront us. There is little expressed emotion here. Yet this reticent quality, together with the secret light of dawn coming over the hills, is sufficient to create a supernatural mood. The dreamlike presence appears as though from the subconscious of the sleeping guards. They, in their inanimate form, represent the world; He, the force that dominates it.

Piero has used his typically hard and sculpturesque modeling for the central figure. The body, flag, and leg are related to the verticality of the trees, while the tomb parallels the horizon line. The composition becomes an arrangement of verticals, horizontals, and diagonals, revolving around the main character toward whom everything turns. The spectator appears to be looking at the picture from slightly below the level of the figures. (The guard facing us is supposed to be Piero himself.)

Although the rising figure of Christ gives a dynamic feeling to that area, the general effect is one of controlled force and, in the lower portion, almost of inaction. The sleeping guards have a certain wooden quality perhaps due to Piero's use of wood or clay figures for models, a practice as common in the fifteenth century as it is today. Others, however, used these figures as starting points; Piero took advantage of their "woodenness" to convey the idol-like immobility which allowed him to concentrate on composition and the illusion of space.

His sculptural qualities are extremely personal and seem almost modern in their concern with methods and techniques, their subordination of emotional effects. Similarly his generalizations of form, although typical for Italian painting, have a streamlined quality that has appealed to many contemporary painters. The geometric manner of relating the foreground, middleground, and background is another particularly modern feature.

Piero is the typical fifteenth-century investigator, representing in his pictures the theories of perspective and proportion about which he later wrote. He and his pupil Luca Pacioli are predecessors of the art theories of Leonardo da Vinci and Albrecht Dürer. Piero, perhaps the greatest explorer of form and space in his time, died on October 12, 1492.

SANDRO BOTTICELLI

(*Alessandro Filipepi*)

BOTTICELLI is one of the great poetic painters—sensitive, withdrawn from the world, interested in the expression of a delicate and exquisite feeling unmatched in his or almost any time. In strong contrast to the sculpturesque scientific method of the Giotto-Masaccio-Piero tradition, Botticelli's work is a gentle, lyrical, poetic style worked out with flat picture surfaces and decorative flowing linear effects. Emotionally it is never brutal or overpowering, but diffident, reserved, subtly suffering.

Botticelli's background was not out of the ordinary; he was the son of a tanner. His name, which means "little barrel," was apparently the nickname of his elder brother, a goldsmith to whom he was apprenticed for a while. From there, however, he went to work in the studio of Fra Lippo Lippi, a tender and gracious portrayer of soft moods in a decorative style. To these poetic qualities Botticelli added a lean vigor and linear power derived from such masters as the Pollaiuoli. By the age of thirty-five his own personal manner of expression was fixed.

At the height of his powers, Botticelli painted the famous *The Birth of Venus* (fig. 7) and *Spring*, pictures expressing the intellectual and nonworldly ideals of the group around Lorenzo the Magnificent, Florence's great patron of the arts. These two pictures are among the most celebrated of the thousands of fifteenth-century paintings.

7 BOTTICELLI   *The Birth of Venus*

Done about 1478 they are characteristic of the Medici's love of finely turned and complicated literary references. Both pictures allude to classical poetry and to contemporary verse. By this means, they make a delicate and obscure allegory of the ill-starred love affair between Giuliano dei Medici and Simonetta Vespucci. In part, this indirection was dictated by the fact that Simonetta was a married woman.

The Birth of Venus is the poet-painter's evocation of the birth of the goddess of love out of the sea. In a remote and self-absorbed way she stands on a cockleshell, blown shoreward by breezes represented by the figures at the left. The semicircular composition is completed by the clothed woman at the right who eagerly waits to receive the nude goddess. In spite of this arrangement, the picture is not balanced in the monumental Masaccio manner; it is, rather, a series of twisting, turning lines and forms. The painter is not interested in stressing three-dimensional or sculptural quality, but rather in evoking emotional effect, through the restlessness of outline and mood.

The movement begins with the intertwined forms of the breezes as they fly toward the right, their draperies blowing wildly and wings tensely arched. It continues with the deliberately off-centered figure of Venus and her curling snakelike hair. Finally it ends in the forward-moving, draped woman and the sinuously curved, almost metallic covering she holds ready for the goddess. The eye of the spectator follows the restless curving lines and constantly changing movement from one side to the other and from top to bottom. Although Venus is the central figure the artist has placed her far enough to the right to help lead us in that direction. Nor is she the dramatic center of the work, for the energetic breezes and the eager young woman at the right are just as significant.

The preoccupied mood of the Venus here and in the *Spring* reflects not only the disillusionment and abstraction resulting from the hidden love story, but the introspective and spiritual approach of the artist as well. The love was unfulfilled, for Giuliano dei Medici had been assassinated only a short time before by political conspirators. The obscure and allegorical way of referring to this tragic affair suited the taste of the Medici circle. Here toward the end of the fifteenth century a conscious attempt was made to evoke the beauty and pagan mystery of the past by intellectuals who felt that money and power had come to occupy their countrymen too much. In various ways they were fleeing from the increasing materialism of the period.

The Medici themselves were a family originally of the merchant class. After a few generations of political leadership in Florence they tended to take on the genteel and elegant manners of the aristocracy. Their patronage of men like Botticelli, Fra Lippo Lippi, Michelangelo, and many literary figures followed this pattern. Botticelli was not a popular favorite; the taste of the forward-moving middle class of the period was best represented in the latter part of the century by a narrative and chatty sort of painting found in Ghirlandajo and others.

The aristocratic quality implied in *The Birth of Venus* or in the linear and elegant *Portrait of a Youth* (color plate I) is also expressed in such religious works as the celebrated *Madonna of the Magnificat* (fig. 8). This is named after the phrase which she has written: *"Magnificat anima mea dominum"* (My soul glorifies the Lord!). The Latin words are scarcely reflected in the moody sensuous beauty posed as the Madonna or in the gracious aristocratic poses and gestures of the courtiers. Here Botticelli has brought together his typical angular, firmly outlined faces, his sinuously flowing contour lines. In this tondo (from the Italian rotondo or round) all the forms are subordinated to the two-dimensional circular rhythm of the frame, and to the special poetic mood that is Botticelli's province.

8   BOTTICELLI   *Madonna of the Magnificat*

JAN VAN EYCK

ONE of the greatest masters of Flemish painting, Jan van Eyck reflects the special character of the fifteenth-century Netherlands which at that time included both Holland and Flanders, or Belgium. He sums up their peculiar mixture of piety and worldliness, their balance of aristocratic and middle class elements, their feeling for pageant-like brilliance, rich colors and splendid materials. Van Eyck worked for both merchant and lord, creating fine religious paintings as well as distinguished and highly detailed portraits. As court painter to the Duke of Burgundy, he occupied a unique place at the Duke's headquarters in Bruges and even acted as his ambassador on several secret missions. When van Eyck went to Spain, his fame was such that his pictures commanded fabulous prices; we are told they brought their actual weight in gold—a sizable sum, since most of them were done on heavy wooden panels.

Why were these works so highly cherished? According to her will, an Italian woman of that century who left a Flemish painting to her parish church considered this picture her most precious possession "because it is so pious." Every aspect of the late medieval art of Flanders is suffused with religious feeling and solemnity. Moreover, the paintings have an enamel-like surface giving an almost jeweled effect; the particularly shiny and transparent quality is due to the use of a then newly developed oil-and-egg emulsion. Above all, however, the works of such great Flemish masters as Jan van Eyck and Rogier van der Weyden employ strange and very effective symbols. In this "transfigured symbolism," ordinary everyday objects achieve an unusual significance which must have intrigued the Spaniards and Italians of the time. A shiny bowl and clean towel may represent the purity of the Virgin, and a lighted candle may signify the presence of God in an Annunciation or other sacred scene. Thus the Flemish masters bring the divine closer to the earthly and the everyday closer to the sacred.

Flemish pictures like the *Madonna of Chancellor Rolin* (fig. 9) usually are far more detailed than the broadly done Italian paintings, and their space arrangements are spread out rather than centralized. They avoid the single concentration point of the Italians and instead use a series of points toward which lines are made to converge. Similarly, Flemish painters are not interested in a single emotional impact, but present areas of piled-up details each one of which can often make a picture of itself.

From the two figures with their vividly colored garments, our eyes follow the converging floor lines to the deeper space in the picture—to the two tiny figures leaning over the parapet and looking into the water, and beyond them to the panorama of the city. Rather than a single point toward which all lines lead—as they would in an Italian painting—there is a series of focal points on an imaginary vertical line through the center of the picture. The floor lines meet at one spot, the line from the Chancellor's book goes to a higher place on the imaginary vertical, and the lines coming from the tops of the columns converge at a still higher point. All of this tilts the picture toward the spectator in a systematic space system which has its own rules. Additional spatial quality appears in the landscape treatment and is made possible by the new transparent oil-and-egg medium.

The Arnolfini Marriage (fig. 10) shows van Eyck's symbolism on another level. It presents an Italian banker resident in Bruges, with the Flemish bride he has just taken. He holds her hand in a solemn gesture of public acknowledgment as demanded of a foreigner by custom. To under-

9   JAN VAN EYCK   *Madonna of Chancellor Rolin*

10   JAN VAN EYCK   *The Arnolfini Marriage*

line this public avowal, the painter has written his signature on the rear wall above the convex mirror: "Jan van Eyck was here." But the painter is not the only witness. In the lighted candle overhead he has symbolized the presence of God. Other everyday objects give sacred meaning to the scene. The wooden clogs in the foreground have been taken off, again to indicate the holiness of the moment.

The room is filled with atmosphere that seems so real as to be almost tangible. This atmospheric effect is a constant feature of Netherlands painting. Along with the luminous detail and highly polished finish of the various objects, it turns up once more in Dutch painters of the seventeenth century like Vermeer.

Van Eyck's *Annunciation* (color plate II) has this tangible atmosphere, as well as brilliant reds and blues made possible by the new paint medium. The old Romanesque architecture resembles that of the Rolin picture. Whenever van Eyck portrays his Madonna within a cathedral, he creates a strange kind of proportion between the height of the Virgin and that of the stone columns. Here the enlargement of the figures makes them take on a supernatural impressiveness as their heads rise almost to the tops of the columns and finally dominate even the church itself.

ROGIER VAN DER WEYDEN

THE art of Rogier van der Weyden, widely copied in his own land and time, became one of the important foundations of later northern European painting. After Jan van Eyck's death, the job of court painter to the Duke of Burgundy was taken over by van der Weyden who had been the "city painter" of Brussels for many years. Although he was the son of a sculptor, his linear art is definitely opposed to the broad realistic effects which van Eyck had achieved in his draperies. In fact, he differs from that master in most respects. Between them, they represent the two chief trends of the Flemish school in the fifteenth century. However, van Eyck's subtle atmospheric qualities and careful piling up of detail were difficult to copy and resulted in a relatively slim following. The linear style of van der Weyden was more immediately influential.

Rogier's first masterpiece, the famous *The Descent from the Cross* (fig. 11) shows his personal style fully developed. This is perhaps the most extraordinary *Descent* in the whole range of art. In spite of the curious formalism and careful balance of effects, it arouses the deepest feelings of pity. Rogier has set up his figures as a two-dimensional relief carved in wood against a broad niche-like background. The design moves from the tragic, fainting Mary supported by St. John across the lowered body of Christ, to the richly dressed Joseph of Arimathea, ending finally in the sorrowing Magdalen. Strong linear parallels organize the flat surface. The balanced outward curves of St. John and the Magdalen bracket the main action, and are repeated in the straight lines of the man and the woman immediately adjacent to them. Most effective are the parallel curved bodies of Christ and the fainting Virgin, their left arms held up and their right arms hanging limply down. Each side has its own compositional effect based on the arrangement of three figures dominated by a curving form.

Rogier's mature style as shown in this remarkable altarpiece is linear or graphic rather than sculpturesque, its figures flat rather than rounded, its outlook pathetic rather than serene and calm. All these qualities differentiate it sharply from the work of Jan van Eyck. It is a kind of abstract emotionalism, very modern in some respects with religious pathos as its chief substance.

Rogier's figures, like the bending St. John and the Magdalen in figure 11, tend to move across and not into the picture space. They also take on a curious, somewhat agitated motion, especially in the drapery. John's cloak flutters back behind him as he bends to perform his act of mercy. His movement is not actually swift enough for this to happen, but by indicating such a fluttering effect the artist conveys a spiritual unrest which is typical of the north European, or Gothic art of the period. This linear sensitivity may be compared in a general way with that of Botticelli, but there is little Gothic agitation in the Italian artist, who was impelled by altogether different emotional motives. Yet it might be observed that Flemish, like Italian fifteenth-century painting shows two parallel styles: the sculptural and the linear.

The particular sensitivity of line that is characteristic of Rogier appears on another level in the restrained and solemn quality of his fine portraits. A typically tiny panel, the *Portrait of a Lady* (fig. 12), shows the remarkable combination of abstract form and psychological penetration of which Rogier was capable. There is nothing here of the involved and pathetic gestures seen in *The Descent from the Cross*.

The body as a whole is flattened and, together with gar-

11 ROGIER VAN DER WEYDEN
The Descent from the Cross

National Gallery of Art, Washington, D. C. (Mellon Collection

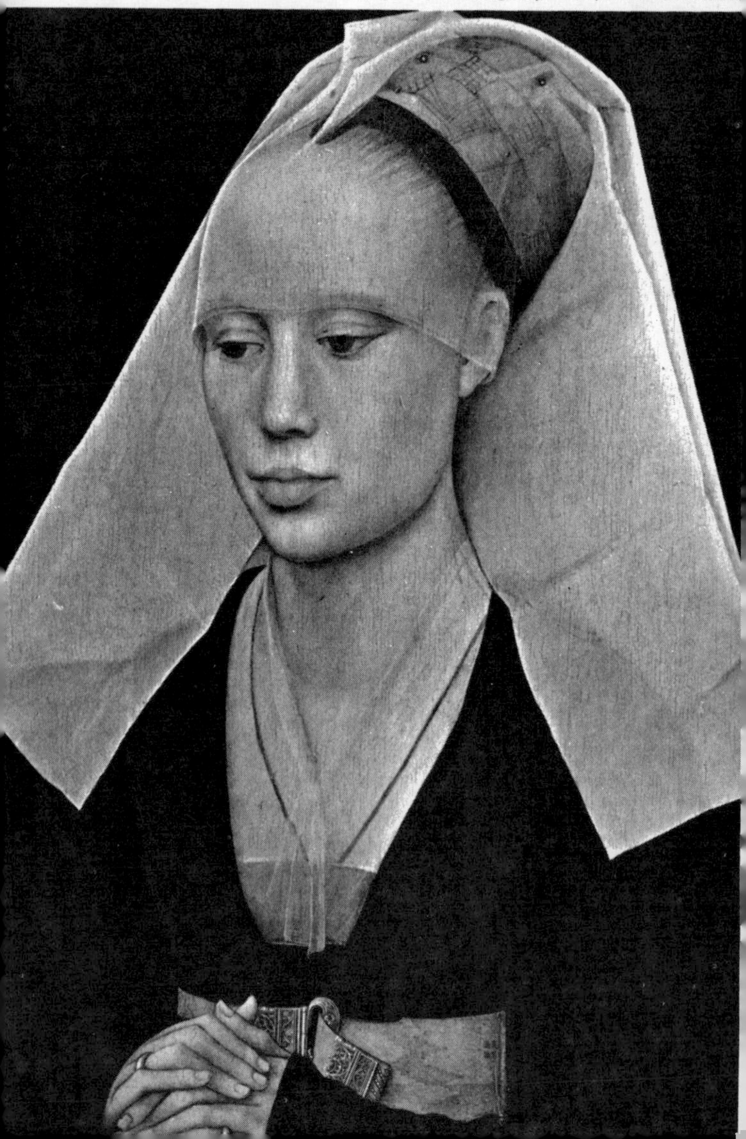

ments and jewels, is reduced to a linear pattern. The gentle curves of the eyes and lips are related to the shape of the face generally and to the swelling openings of the nose; the angular spread of the white coif enframes the oval collar and coat openings. All of these forms emphasize the outline, the sensitively moving linear pattern. Although the eyes look away, they indicate a feeling for the character of the sitter. This sensitivity is far from the mannerism it became in many later portraits. There is a strange contrast between this gentility and, for instance, the famous smile of the *Mona Lisa.*

Rogier's influence was very extensive. The outward characteristics of his linear conventions lent themselves to imitation, in his own time, by innumerable people in Holland and Belgium. Later, German painters and engravers like Schongauer and Dürer (figs. 21, 22), and even Italian painters, like Cosimo Tura, felt the impact of his strange, abstract, linear style.

12 ROGIER VAN DER WEYDEN *Portrait of a Lady*

LEONARDO DA VINCI

UNQUESTIONABLY the most glittering personality of the High Renaissance in Italy and the pioneer in its new and magnificent form of expression was Leonardo da Vinci. Even as a youth he displayed an aptitude for all manner of achievement, a winning charm, and a personal strength and beauty which have become almost legendary. In time this brilliant boy would become not only one of the leading artists of the early sixteenth century, but its greatest contributor to the advancement of modern ideas as well. Leonardo possessed a variety of artistic talents—he was architect, sculptor, musician. He also mastered and did original work in the fields of mathematics, geology, engineering, anatomy, and every other science known in his day. More than anyone else he had "taken all knowledge as his sphere." The ideal Renaissance man, he represented that spirit of inquiry which expressed itself so well in the investigations of his fellow artists.

Before Leonardo, there had been two parallel trends in Italian painting: the monumental scientific side represented by Masaccio and Piero della Francesca; and the more decorative, linear, and poetic side expressed in Botticelli. Leonardo achieved a combination of these two trends. His impressive idealized forms are worked out with every consideration for scientific knowledge, and yet seem surrounded by an aura of poetic sentiment.

Unfortunately, he was too busy with a host of other projects to finish many pictures. One of the greatest of the

13 LEONARDO DA VINCI *Madonna of the Rocks*

few he left is the *Madonna of the Rocks* (fig. 13). Here, in one painting, are the qualities that make Leonardo a typical artist of the late or High Renaissance: an increasingly idealized portrayal of human beings, and a formal, mathematical arrangement of the persons in the picture. Leonardo, like many other masters of this period, presents a kind of superbeing nobly formed and quietly expressive. (In the work of each artist there is a distinct variety of this idealized type that may be called Leonardesque, Raphaelesque, etc.) The conception of the children in this picture, the gently smiling angel and the otherworldly Madonna, all contribute a feeling of more than human nobility and perfection to the new classicism of that age. The figures move in a dignified, restrained way; their gestures have a solemnity and poise that are seldom found in ordinary people. This is the classical line laid down by Giotto and Masaccio, now reaching new and more expressive levels.

The most characteristic device of almost all High Renaissance artists is to fit the figures into a specific geometrical pattern: a pyramid in this conception of the Madonna, a circle in the Botticelli picture (fig. 8), or a parallelogram in the Raphael (fig. 18). This gives a systematic and ordered quality to the works of the High Renaissance which is different from the individual monumentality emphasized by painters during the early fifteenth century. (See Masaccio's *The Expulsion from Paradise* [fig. 4].) The artists themselves in this later period are even more individualistic than those of the earlier Renaissance, but the ideas they represent are wider than those of the little city-states for which Piero, Masaccio, and others had worked. During this age, when Italian nationalism first appeared through the political activities of the papacy, art went beyond its former local expressions in search of universal values.

Leonardo spent the early part of his life in Florence and then stayed in Milan for a number of years working on many important projects, including the *Madonna of the Rocks* and the *Last Supper*. The latter (perhaps the best known painting in the world) offers one of the finest in-

stances of a rigid geometric enclosure. Everything turns inward toward the head of Christ, even the expressive gestures of His own hands. In spite of the great excitement within the work, complete formal control is maintained.

The balance of geometric organization and realistic emotion in the *Last Supper* as in the *Madonna of the Rocks* and the *Mona Lisa* (fig. 14) is only one part of the story. In addition we must note, especially in the last two pictures, the characteristic Leonardo fusion of the monumental and scientific approach with a lyrical feeling. In the *Madonna of the Rocks,* sculpturesque and largely conceived figures are surrounded by minute and accurately recorded details of rock formations and flower forms seen in the neighborhood of Milan. On the other hand, there is a sense of mystery and poetry that comes from the other major trend in Italian art. This is the Botticelli magic which Leonardo has transformed with his mysterious background, waterfall, and his own brand of thoughtful absorption in the face of the Madonna.

In the *Mona Lisa,* one of the most overdiscussed and overrated pictures of all time (through no fault of its own), the same balance of monumental form and lyrical feeling is clearly evident. This poetic sense, here as in many other works, is a definite Leonardo quality. It has little to do with portraiture, that is, with analysis of the sitter. If it is considered part of the painter's own personality and not that of the somewhat smug lady, the picture takes on a different meaning. Certainly it is mysterious, but so are Leonardo's other paintings. To this artist, all things, human and divine, were fit subjects for the searching analysis of his extraordinary mind.

MICHELANGELO
BUONARROTI

THE turbulent spirit of Michelangelo expressed itself in an unceasing lifelong production of great sculpture and paintings. But in spite of the vast force and violent movement expressed in his gigantic forms, he maintained the typical High Renaissance balance of power and control, and he preserved his own quality of thoughtfulness.

Like Leonardo, Michelangelo was a many-sided artist. He was outstanding as an architect, sculptor, and painter; he wrote poetry and occasionally engaged in engineering. His most vital activity, however, was in the field of sculpture, a fact which is clearly reflected in the very character of his painting.

Michelangelo was born and brought up in Florence, and reacted to the same stimuli as the other artists of that center. Like them he spent much time in the Brancacci Chapel studying the frescoes of Masaccio. And there, in response to a taunt, another student smashed his nose, disfiguring him for life. As he developed, the young Michelangelo turned from technical experiments toward more general forms in which knowledge of anatomy, perspective, and other devices could be taken for granted. The chief influence on his early life came from an association with the Medici family. Through these great art patrons, he came into contact with philosophers and poets as well as artists. As a Medici protégé, he first learned the rudiments of sculpture in their academy.

15 MICHELANGELO *The Creation of Adam*

Sistine Chapel, Vatican, Rome (Anderson)

At the age of thirty Michelangelo was called to Rome, and for the next thirty years he worked there for a succession of Popes. Apart from the unfinished tomb for Pope Julius II, which was to have been his masterpiece in sculpture, the most important work of this period is the magnificent and elaborate painting on the ceiling of the Sistine Chapel in the Vatican. This immense ceiling, almost an acre in area, is forty feet above the ground, curved in form and interrupted by window openings. It would have been a tremendous problem to any experienced painter. For Michelangelo, who had as yet done very little painting, certainly nothing on an overhead surface, it was a formidable challenge.

First he had to decide on an appropriate subject for the chapel itself and for the particular space to be covered, and then a workable scheme of decoration that would not be monotonous in so large a space. The theme chosen was the creation of the world, of man and woman, their fall from grace and the destruction of the Flood. The Redemption is foreshadowed through Old Testament prophets, pagan prophetesses, Biblical scenes of mercy, and the various ancestors of Christ. Michelangelo had to work from a high platform, lying flat on his back with the paint dripping down onto his face. Food was sent up and the artist seems to have descended only to sleep. So intensive and absorbing were his efforts that he rarely changed his clothes and, on one occasion, it is said, tried to remove his boots only to find that his skin had stuck to the leather.

In the center of the rectangular Sistine ceiling, he projected the scenes of the first seven days. Perhaps the best known of these is *The Creation of Adam* (fig. 15) in which God is dramatically portrayed as He comes plunging through the firmament, accompanied by supporting angels, to touch into life the gigantic form of Adam lying on a bare hillock. All the figures are far more than life-size in order to be seen at such a height. The balance between the dynamic movement of the Creator and the passive and relaxed power of the giant human provides a typical High

Renaissance effect, although Michelangelo's control devices are less formal than those of other masters. Adam's body curves downward in a remarkably expressive sweep. He waits with his outstretched arm resting on his knee for the spark from the hand of God to jump the tiny gap between the onrushing force of the Creator and his own limp fingers. The contrast between active power and relaxation is repeated in the similar opposition between the fiery expression on the face of God and the yearning glance of the still inanimate man.

Where Leonardo uses a soft shadow to model his forms, Michelangelo depends primarily on the tense strength of his line. Where Leonardo gives us picturesque, beautiful backgrounds, Michelangelo projects his scene against a bare, almost primeval background. The stage is left clear for the human and divine protagonists in the drama of the moment. Color plays a small part in his works; the sculpturesque form and forceful gesture interest him more than anything else.

Accessory figures are found in great profusion on the Sistine ceiling. Decorative nudes surround each rectangular panel in an infinite variety of positions. Arranged in straight rows along the sides, the main Old Testament prophets alternate with prophetesses or sibyls of antiquity. An elaborate architectural setting is painted around each one, giving the illusion of a giant sculpture placed within a niche. *The Prophet Jeremiah* (fig. 16) is one of the most expressive; the bent shoulders and general downward movement symbolize the sadness of this great seer who sits, chin in hand and eyes half closed, revealing his thoughtful dejection. Most masters of the High Renaissance were able to express the emotions of their figures through positions of the arms and legs or postures of the body; they attached as much importance to these factors as to the expression on the face itself. This is as true of *Jeremiah* as of Adam in the *Creation* scene, Leonardo's *Madonna of the Rocks,* or Raphael's *School of Athens.*

What is especially striking—and characteristic of Michel-

HIEREMIAS

16   MICHELANGELO   *The Prophet Jeremiah*

angelo—in the portrayal of this heroically built prophet is the illusion of a three-dimensional space in which the figure can actually move. This is effected through the powerful contour line of the form itself, and the painted recess of the niche in which it is set. Jeremiah's legs are drawn in under him, implying the same possibility of movement as do the hunched shoulders and sunken head.

When the monumental painting in the Sistine Chapel was finished, it was signed: "Michelangelo, Sculptor."

RAPHAEL

(Raffaello Santi)

In some ways Raphael is the most typical master of the High Renaissance. Without the turbulent personality of Michelangelo, he represents the most serene and self-confident aspect of that brief age of glory. In his short life of thirty-seven years, he summed up the assurance of the era as well as its many worldly, artistic, and intellectual accomplishments.

From a material point of view, Raphael's life was a continuous series of triumphs, mounting from one success to another. After a modest provincial background at Urbino he went to the art center of Florence and ended in the great cosmopolitan Rome of the Renaissance Popes. Artistically, his development repeats the evolution of Italian art up to his own time. From an early cramped sentimentalism his work moves to a more monumental Florentine style, and finally to the serene classical assurance of the Roman works. Intellectually, he reflects the urge of his time toward a compromise between the classical past and the Christian present.

The conventional and typical side of Raphael's art may be seen in the many charming Madonnas which present his own brand of sentiment as well as the characteristic preferences of the period as a whole. These works have remained popular for more than four hundred years. The familiar *The Alba Madonna* (fig. 17), is a *tondo* or round picture in which the three figures are neatly arranged in a parallelogram within the circle of the frame. One straight line may be traced along the Madonna's leg and the arm holding the book; on the other side a parallel line moves from Her left shoulder to the hip of little St. John the Baptist. The short sides of this typical geometric enclosure are formed by the left upper arm and by the line from the tip of Her extended foot to the hip of St. John. The body of the Christ Child forms a second parallelogram placed at an angle to the first.

In contrast to this strict symmetry, the three faces express a yearning sentimentality, probably intended to give a mystical feeling to the picture, much favored in certain circles for its clear religious character. This scene of unworldliness, heightened by the isolated and almost empty landscape, is a prominent feature of the Neo-Platonic idealism of the period. Some of the elements are reminiscent of Michelangelo (the hand holding the book) or Leonardo (the forms and faces of the children), but the synthesis is Raphael's own. This is illustrated again in his sentimental *St. George and the Dragon* (color plate III) which is arranged in an "X" shape that moves into the four corners of the picture.

The literary and intellectual side of the Renaissance, its fusion of classical and Christian elements, may be seen in the series of frescoes executed for Pope Julius II in the papal apartments of the Vatican. Here, all the knowledge of the day, pagan and Christian, has been brought together. *The School of Athens* (fig. 18), one of the best known sections of these splendid decorations shows the philosophers, scientists, and poets of the ancient Greek world moving through the nave of a cathedral very much like St. Peter's (then in process of rebuilding). The painting on the wall opposite is a summary of Christian theology.

In the *School* various persons are arranged in a rectangle that occupies the lower half of the wall. A series of receding space areas carries the spectator in and up to the lofty vaults that move into the distance, giving the scene an

17 RAPHAEL *The Alba Madonna*

18

RAPHAEL
*The School
of Athens*

Raphael Rooms,
Vatican, Rome
(Anderson)

effect of profound depth. In the exact center are Plato and
Aristotle, the two philosophers who represent the ideal and
the practical sides of life. Plato, who resembles the elderly
Leonardo da Vinci, points upward in a spiritual gesture;
Aristotle holds his hand straight out with the palm facing
down toward the earth. Similarly the figures at the left
represent philosophical learning (like the gesticulating
Socrates on the top step) while those on the right represent
more practical learning (like Euclid in the lower corner
demonstrating a theorem).

The frescoes in this series are notable not only because
Raphael has brought together a tremendous body of knowledge, but also because the arrangement of forms is balanced
and controlled in such a seemingly easy and comfortable
way. In *The School of Athens* the eye is directed to the central figures and the deep space beyond them with absolute
inevitability. The floor lines and the figures on them (including the skeptical Diogenes sprawling on the stairs)
lead to the steps; the eye is carried to the next important
level by Diogenes and the man walking up near him. At
the top of the steps there is a short halt. The figures here
are arranged in a straight line as though in relief sculpture;
the eye moves out to the corners and then in again to the
central figures under their arch. The next move is up into
the vaults, each one constituting a point of rest with the
alternating empty spaces. Each set of vault lines moves
closer together until they ultimately converge at a point
between the two main philosophers. Thus the many figures
and the spacious architecture inevitably return to the central point of the painter's argument where the elderly Plato
holds his book of *Ethics* and the young vigorous Aristotle
carries his *Politics*—the two perfect symbols of the theoretical and practical approaches.

The latter part of Raphael's short life was filled with a
variety of work. He was directing architect of St. Peter's
and other building projects; he was in charge of archaeological excavations in the entire Roman area; and he supervised—less and less closely—the many commissions which

poured into his studio. One of the most popular figures of his period, he was widely courted both as an artist and as a man. Untroubled, he fulfilled countless social obligations, proved endlessly fascinating to the ladies, and somehow managed to maintain control of his many projects. Eventually the pace began to tell on both his health and his work; but to his countrymen he remained "the lucky boy." He died on Good Friday of 1520 and was buried in the ancient Roman Pantheon which had been converted into a church.

TITIAN

(*Tiziano Vecellio*)

THE art of Venice has a splendor of its own that is different from the eloquent painting of Rome during the High Renaissance. The works of men like Titian have a more sensuous, sparkling quality that expresses the luxurious and pleasureful pageantry of the picturesque port on the Adriatic. This city, already involved in the wars that hastened its decay, was still one of the most important commercial centers in the world. It stood at the crossroads between the East and the West, reflecting a magnificence and love of display entirely distinct from the rest of Italy. Whereas the art of Rome and Florence was intellectual, that of Venice was a combination of the material and the poetic; whereas the former relied mainly on precise drawing for its effects, the art of Venice depended on bright and glowing colors.

Like most Venetian painters, Titian was not born in Venice. The charming landscapes found in the background of many of his works recall his childhood in the country. Personally, he seems less than admirable in his undisguised hunger for money and power, his flattery of the many noble clients who sat to him for portraits, and his willingness to associate with people like the blackmailer, Pietro Aretino, who was able to give him a good deal of favorable publicity. Yet in these very qualities Titian revealed himself a man of his time and his city, the money-minded Queen of the Adriatic.

His early works were done under the influence of the poetic Giorgione, his fellow pupil in the studio of Giovanni Bellini. These paintings have a gentle, lyrical, and sentimental quality that is exemplified by the famous *Sacred and Profane Love* in the Palazzo Borghese in Rome. During his second period, Titian turned toward a more vigorous statement of the beauties of love, of friendship, and of motherhood, and produced splendid unpoetical portrayals of religious, classical, and other themes. These paintings, in their rich rendition of materials and their straightforward presentation of people's feelings, are among his best works.

In 1533 Titian met the Emperor Charles; it was a command performance. He was made a knight (and later a count) and was constantly occupied with painting pictures of the Emperor and his family. Now he became less exuberant and more objective, more impersonal and official in his outlook. This is particularly evident in the many portraits of important personages of the time: kings, princes, noblemen, beautiful women. They are all treated with a sense of distinction—and perhaps flattery—that has left an ineradicable imprint on the course of official portrait painting ever since.

The portrait of *Pietro Aretino* (fig. 19) presents the prize scandalmonger and poison-pen writer of the period. As a good friend of the painter, however, he emerges here with a serene calm and objectivity that belie the man's reputation and activities. This ill-tempered and sensual author of threatening letters (whom Michelangelo once told off in no uncertain terms) appears in impressive bulk. He is placed in the picture space not by virtue of tight draughtsmanship but rather through transparent layers of oil paint, one over another, which absorb or reflect light as the painter chooses. When the light is allowed to penetrate a thin outer paint to the dark under-paint, the effect is a dark area or a shadow; when the light is not allowed to penetrate a thicker surface layer, it shines back into the eye of the spectator and causes a light area. Painting in broad sure strokes and de-emphasizing details, the artist

19 TITIAN *Pietro Aretino*

achieves an impression of genuine three-dimensionality and volume. While the fabrics of the clothing are not done in detail, they are rendered with a regard for their actual quality as materials.

Instead of showing the colossal self-assurance and brutality of this individual from whose friendship he has profited, Titian leaves an illusion of benign wisdom. If he did as well for his other clients, we can begin to understand the great popularity of this master. Wherever we compare his interpretation of a person with that given by another painter—as in the case of Francis I who was also painted by the Clouet family in France—we can see why there was rivalry for the privilege of sitting to Titian.

The more directly sensual and ostentatious side of Titian's art may be seen in the *Venus and the Lute Player* (fig. 20). In this late work (c. 1562–65), the delicacy and richness of Titian's color reaches a new height with its sensitive glazes and surface mixings of paint. The broad sweeping lines of the composition carry the eye from side to side in a semicircle reaching from the little Cupid at the right to the tip of the musician's lute and up into the mountains at the left. The nude Venus and the young poetic nobleman seem to have been interrupted in the course of playing music. She holds a flute in her hand and the young man turns from his lute to watch the little godling place a crown of love on her head. There is a feeling of things having stopped, of sounds hovering in the air, the poetic inheritance of Titian's earlier life. But this voluptuous and richly portrayed woman is far from a poetic type—not because she may to our eyes look somewhat overabundant, but rather because the painter looks upon her in too matter-of-fact a way. She is a magnificent still life, a beautifully and materialistically handled piece of flesh, rich and splendid like the red curtains in the background with their warm shadows.

Perhaps the most effective part of the picture is the landscape background. It is as light and atmospheric, as spontaneously poetic as that of any artist of the centuries following; the course was charted in this and similar works by Titian. Here are Poussin and Rembrandt, Watteau, Fragonard, Gainsborough, Constable, and perhaps even Cézanne—all those who interested themselves in the delicate transition from tone to tone which gives the illusion of depth in nature. Similarly, Titian's *Venus with a Mirror* (color plate IV) is reflected in theme by Rembrandt and Rubens, in rich fleshliness and tight composition by Renoir.

Until the age of ninety-nine when he died of the plague, Titian was still vigorous, still pointing the way to the future.

20   TITIAN   *Venus and the Lute Player*   Courtesy of the Metropolitan Museum of Art, New York

ALBRECHT DÜRER

DURING the early Protestant Reformation no school of northern European painting was as important as the German, and no painter as important as Albrecht Dürer. Apart from his accomplishments in oil painting, Dürer is perhaps the outstanding master of the engraving and woodcut. His sketches of animal and plant life in watercolor, pencil, and pen suggest similar works by Leonardo da Vinci; his studies of perspective and proportion compare in significance with those of the Italians.

Both as man and artist, Dürer typifies the conflicts of his time and country. Germany was then emerging from the Middle Ages into the Renaissance, and was very much aware of its role in breaking away from the Catholic Church. Thus, although considered "ambassador of the Italian Renaissance" to the north, Dürer's work shows both the serene humanism and form of the Italians, and the conflicting stream of the native Gothic reaction against worldliness as well.

Born in Nürnberg into a family of goldsmiths, Dürer went through the typical apprenticeship of the period, spent some time wandering about the country, and then returned to Nürnberg, married and settled down to work. Unfortunately his wife, although beautiful, had a nagging temperament which made life a sore trial.

Dürer's first trip to Venice in 1495 apparently had little influence on the detailed linear style he inherited from Flemish painting of the fifteenth century. His second visit

21 DÜRER *The Adoration of the Magi*

22 DÜRER *Hieronymus Holzschuher*
Kaiser Friedrich Museum, Berlin

to Venice in 1505 was made partly to protect his engravings from being pirated, and partly to enlarge his artistic horizons. The influence this time is abundantly clear. In Italy, as he wrote to his friends, he found himself appreciated far more than at home. More important, his contacts with the painters of the Renaissance had a permanent effect on his art.

The well-known *The Adoration of the Magi* (fig. 21) illustrates the typical mixture of Gothic-German and Renaissance-Italian ideas in Dürer's art. We can recognize, for example, the Leonardo pyramid seen earlier in the *Madonna of the Rocks* (fig. 13). The elderly king kneeling before the Christ Child is "lifted" from Leonardo's *Adoration* in the Uffizi Gallery, as is the motif of the rearing horses in the rear. The Wise Man at the right stands in a graceful pose characteristic of many Italian figures.

In spite of these and other identifiable Renaissance elements, however, Dürer's picture remains both German and personal because of its tremendous detail and meticulous craftsmanship. The generalized form found in Italian painting is swamped by an abundance of ornament, jewelry, and embroidery. Marvelous little still-life pictures of flowers and insects (lower left), animal and other life (lower right) also appear through the magic of his microscopic engraver's treatment. Leonardo put similar small items into his *Madonna of the Rocks*, and for the same scientific reasons which inspired Dürer, but the net result is quite different. In the Italian painting the detail, however loving, is subordinated to the general effect, while here the detail is often just as important as the whole.

In common with the painters of Italy, Dürer is very much concerned with problems of recession in space. In this *Adoration*, the pyramid formed by the figures actually comes to a point some distance back, at the top of a tree. Similarly, converging lines recede into the picture, at right angles to the protagonists who are arranged across the picture space. Dürer has constructed a rather elaborate manger, since he is interested not only in the scene as such, but in the possibilities of composition and perspective.

The kings, it is true, were borrowed from various places, but it is significant that the Madonna is not at all an Italian type. Although the mature form repeats the Venetian Madonnas the face is German. Dürer's portraits show the same mingling of Italian and Germanic elements.

His famous interpretation of the scholar *Hieronymus Holzschuher*, (fig. 22) only two years before the painter's death, is one of the finest portraits in German art. It shows the powerful and monumental form of Italian painting and, in addition, the minute detail and the emotional agitation of his own tradition. Holzschuher was painted after the beginning of the Reformation, a time of strain on old habits and loyalties; he has a definitely disturbed and unhappy look. Technically, this mood has been achieved by bringing the eyes of the subject to the right, exposing the whites to a certain extent, and giving the face a rather wild quality. This emotive portrait differs in its detailed rendering of beard, hair, and other features from the generalized and self-confident pictures of the Italians; it also differs in offering a completely nonflattering image. This man, like Titian's *Pietro Aretino* (fig. 19), was a good friend of the painter. Yet the Italian work is a surface and objective treatment whose purpose seems to be flattery, while the German painting is a deep subjective study of the character of this wise and good man.

In 1520 the ever-curious Dürer made a trip into the Netherlands. He was received like a prince, lived in splendid style, and was given all possible honors. More important, this journey helped turn the painters and engravers of the Low Countries toward the Renaissance. As in his own land, Dürer carried this influence into new and fertile areas.

HANS HOLBEIN
THE YOUNGER

HOLBEIN belongs to a generation that saw the full flowering of the Protestant Reformation, the end of the High Renaissance, and the growth of centralized monarchies in France, England, Germany, and Spain. The artistic influences that came to him from the south were now more artificial and formal than those which had affected Dürer. Italian art had changed from the self-confident High Renaissance style to the courtly, precise, and often strained manner of the courts of this later time.

Born in Augsburg, Germany, into a family of artists, the younger Holbein had grown up in a prosperous environment which was very favorable to art. After an apprenticeship and years of wandering he settled in Basel, Switzerland where much of his work may still be seen.

It was not until he painted the *Madonna of Mayor Meyer* (fig. 23) that Holbein really found himself. This impressive and dignified representation shows the Meyer family at the feet of the Virgin who is framed in a classical conch shell. Here Holbein continues the Italian tradition initiated by Dürer, but with far less of the detailed Gothic manner. The gentle, fair charm of the Madonna, the blond loveliness of the Child, and the aristocratic quality of the young courtier in the foreground (compare fig. 8 by Botticelli) suggest the finest religious painting of Renaissance Italy.

There are differences, however. Germanic rather than

Italian facial types and costumes are used. The feeling of seriousness is in the Flemish tradition, from which German art derived so much of its emotive element. Moreover, this work, like many post-Renaissance portraits, no longer bears the same air of assurance as is found, for instance, in the *Pietro Aretino* (fig. 19). The space quality, so deep and extensive in Italian painting, tends more and more to be flattened and cramped. In Holbein, and in most of the sixteenth-century formalist and court painters, the human figure is increasingly treated as a decorative rather than a three-dimensional object. It becomes part of a carefully arranged flat design rather than a rounded form like the *Aretino*.

The intellectual environment of Basel did Holbein a great deal of good, but he was driven away by the growth of Reformation conservatism in religion and the consequent antiartistic attitude. In 1526, at the suggestion of the great humanist scholar Erasmus, he went to England carrying a recommendation to Sir Thomas More, author of the celebrated *Utopia* which Holbein had illustrated. With the backing of Sir Thomas, then Chancellor of England, Holbein soon became an important portrait painter in London, and ultimately court painter to King Henry VIII. From Henry he received a fixed stipend for working on state paintings, including the portraits of foreign ladies whom the much-wedded king thought of marrying. Among these were Christine of Denmark and Anne of Cleves. Other jobs were the many portraits of the king himself, his son Edward VI, the other wives, and also various private commissions for members of the court.

The painting of *Sir Thomas More* (fig. 24) shows the characteristic Holbein balance between interest in the sitter as a psychological problem, and interest in his form as part of a pattern on the picture surface. Here the psychological factor is undoubtedly greater than with many court figures who are treated in terms of their splendid costumes instead of their possible dignity. Considering the nature of the still rather rude Tudor society, it is apparent

24   HANS HOLBEIN, the Younger
Sir Thomas More

23   HANS HOLBEIN, the Younger *Madonna of Mayor Meyer*
Museum, Darmstadt

that Holbein has adopted a formal and official manner of rendering courtly subjects. The artist is the noninterpreting camera eye and does not commit himself to any point of view. In the case of Sir Thomas he is somewhat more personal in quality, since the subject does not require the same kind of uncritical approach. Apart from this, however, the *Sir Thomas* and the many other portraits done by Holbein in England share his typical linear, two-dimensional quality. The emphasis is on contour line rather than on solidity of form. Similarly, the space is telescoped inward and differs sharply from the rich deep spaces of Raphael, Leonardo, or Titian.

A charming reminiscence of Holbein's long term in England is the portrait of little *Edward VI*, (color plate V) the ill-starred son of Henry VIII who succeeded his father for a brief period. He is shown as the baby Prince of Wales, formally dressed in crimson and gold and as serious as the occasion requires. It is interesting to note, incidentally, that this is the little prince who at a slightly later age figures in Mark Twain's delightful story *The Prince and the Pauper*.

Again the emphasis is on surface pattern, in the precise linear indications of gold on red and the equally formalized threads on the gold sleeves. Each part of the little body, moreover, makes some sort of design: the arms moving to the left, the squared-off face with the lines running into it, and so forth. Space, here also, is deliberately restricted, even cramped. The form is slipped into a narrow place between the marble railing and the cold limiting background. Although the portrayal is not a character interpretation of the young child, it is a serious and thoughtful estimate in the general mood of courtly and mannered sixteenth-century portraiture.

TINTORETTO

(*Jacopo Robusti*)

ITALIAN art in all its branches was inevitably affected by the uncertainties of the sixteenth century. The style of Florence became mannered and highly intellectualized. Venice, shocked by the financial catastrophes of the period, clearly revealed its dismay in the troubled expressions that appeared in so many of its portraits. The new melodramatic intensity of Venetian religious painting marks the beginning of a counter-Reformation to combat the Protestant forces that were breaking away from the Church of Rome.

Tintoretto, perhaps better than anyone else, expresses this new restlessness in northern Italy. He was the son of a dyer, and began his career as an apprentice in Titian's studio. His turbulent temperament as a painter, however, soon made him unwelcome. From the very beginning he leaned toward an uncontrolled violence of mood, an intense quality of expression that differentiated him quite sharply from the rather matter-of-fact poetry of his master. Titian's art is filled with the expected luxury and color of Venice and its upper class patrons. Tintoretto's spectacular canvases show new types of forms, a new conception of space, and the use of melodramatic surprise to highlight a distinctly human and even pathetic quality. To the same degree that Titian pleases the eyes and the senses, Tintoretto appeals to the sympathies. In an age of changing values, when old ideals were crumbling, he brought to painting a new theatrical character. Though still expressed in the vocabulary of religious subject matter the drama of the human being became the important thing.

When Titian's self-confident and splendid *Aretino* (fig. 19) is compared with the Tintoretto portrait of *A Venetian Senator* (fig. 25) a tremendous change is immediately apparent. The senator is surely as significant and worldly a figure as Titian's friend, yet his expression reveals no sense of satisfaction in his own importance. His restless gaze moves toward the spectator, to engage attention and to question. The world is perhaps too much with him. Rather than feeling satisfied and easy in mind he is seeking answers for his problems.

The entire color scheme in these works is new and different. Instead of the subtle variations of tone that Titian used to build up form, there are short impetuous brush strokes in broken color that give an impression of form in a crisper and more agitated fashion. The effect is heightened by little areas of white that highlight the various surfaces and lend a movement and emotional intensity which correspond to the mood of the man portrayed. The *Venetian Senator* is shown with his nervous fingers touching the vertical line of fur that carries the eye back to the unhappy face above. He is turned so that his body moves toward the open window where an endless seascape is dotted by boats which move into the picture from the right.

Tintoretto undertook many elaborate decorations in the various churches and public buildings of Venice. The first of these was the moving *Presentation of the Virgin* with its dramatically isolated little figure at the head of the stairs, toward whom everyone looks and points. A few years later he did the famous *Miracle of the Slave* in which the figure of St. Mark swoops down from the sky to stay an execution. By this time Tintoretto had developed an amazing ability to handle crowds in his pictures, to give the sensation of endless motion and excitement, and to focus the attention of the spectator on a small detail that sums up the character of the scene.

25 TINTORETTO *A Venetian Senator*

26 TINTORETTO *The Crucifixion*

In the later *The Crucifixion* (fig. 26), the painter again personalizes the scene in his astonishingly dramatic fashion. The three crucifixes come into the picture diagonally from the right; an equally sharp diagonal moves up from the lower left to the figure of Christ above. In the background, a row of lances and pikes indicates a crowd of Roman soldiers on the other side of the hill, their banner waving lazily in the breeze. The dramatically high sky reveals the forms of the three crucified ones, the executioner on the ladder, and the man directly beneath him. Apart from the bright banner, the only decisive spot of color is the purple robe of Christ, lying on the ground—but color is not Tintoretto's main purpose. Mary, at the lower left, is sustained by the sympathetic John as he gestures toward the Pharisee who is handing the executioner the derisive placard inscribed "INRI" Jesus of Nazareth, King of the Jews.

Here, Tintoretto has brought into being a non-Renaissance type of "open" composition in which parts of the scene are deliberately cut off and many figures are either coming into or going out of the picture. This lends additional excitement to the scene and creates a new kind of space. It implies that the space can go on and on, since there is no specific limitation as in pictures like Leonardo's *Last Supper* which are closed and complete.

The figures, too, have a new quality. The older, more monumental proportion is abandoned and the forms now become thin and elongated. By their very nature they have more action and excitement. Color is used only as necessary, not merely for decoration and visual enrichment, but for pure dramatic quality, to emphasize or de-emphasize as the need arises. The composition is deliberately spasmodic. We may follow the line from the face of the Virgin up through the curved arm of John to the bent arms of the Pharisee and then to the figure on the ladder whose arm brings us finally to the face of Christ. Thus, the design of the painting in its restless movement also helps fulfill the psychological aims of this painter of human pathos.

EL GRECO

(*Domenicos Theotocopoulos*)

IN sixteenth-century Spain the crisis of religious feeling, the striving for mystic oneness with God, was even more sharply felt than in Italy. The Spanish Reformation and counter-Reformation were far more agonized. In the art of El Greco these passions emerge in a startling way.

Born Domenicos Theotocopoulos on the island of Crete, he was later called El Greco, "the Greek," by the Spaniards. He went to Italy as a young man bringing with him memories of the long austere figures of Eastern Christian or Byzantine art. In Venice he was affected by the compositions of Titian and the elongated twisting forms and broken colors of Tintoretto. In Rome it was the powerfully distorted later sculpture of Michelangelo that impressed him, both for its form and its intensely spiritual qualities. Because there was apparently more work for artists outside of Italy, the painter went to Spain around 1576 and settled in Toledo. Spain was then at the height of the counter-Reformation, with its Inquisition dealing harsh punishment to presumable religious offenders.

El Greco's figures are symbolic distortions and elongations to evoke a great religious and mystical response suitable to that particular moment of Spanish history. The country was dominated by the pious zeal of the mournful Philip II (then busy planning his own tomb, the melancholy Escorial), and was affected in no small measure by

the severity of the Inquisition. The Spain of that day reflected a tortured religiosity far exceeding anything elsewhere in Europe. The painting of El Greco catered to this
feeling, either consciously or unconsciously. His work did
not particularly please the taste of a monarch satisfied with
second-rate Italian painters, but the Church, on the other
hand, was his best customer.

The spirit and meaning of El Greco's art may be seen
clearly in the well-known *St. Martin and the Beggar* (color
plate VI). Here, the elongation and pathos of Tintoretto
have been turned to an even more intensive psychological
purpose. The forms are lengthened and twisted even
further; the heads become tiny entities resting on flamelike
bodies. Color also is raised to a more expressive level. In
order to achieve a spiritual rather than a physical effect,
the artist distorts the actual color of the objects and trans-
forms them into mood symbols. Finally, as in most works
of El Greco's maturity, there is a strange otherworldly
space portrayal. The proportions of the figures in relation
to the background are so altered that they seem to loom
formidably over it and almost to absorb it with their great
size.

These thin-faced, elongated individuals are brought together by the cold yellow-green of the cloak which St.
Martin is dividing with the beggar, and by the mutual
glances of their melancholy eyes. They belong to no particular time of day or night; they are fleshless symbols of
mystical yearnings, thin and emaciated aristocrats out of
whom the blood has been drained for the purpose of greater
spiritual expression. The less physical and "ordinary" the
forms, the more it is possible for painters like El Greco
(or modern Expressionists, for that matter) to obtain the
desired psychological quality. St. Martin and his horse
are so impressively large and looming that they seem to
reach up into the very sky itself where grayish clouds part to
make way for them. As is often the case in El Greco's art,
most of the compositional elements seem to emphasize the
upward movement.

If the St. Martin picture is representative of his figure compositions, the *View of the City of Toledo* (fig. 27) is typical of the painter's treatment of nature. El Greco's name is permanently associated with the ancient city of Toledo where his house, the *Casa del Greco*, still exists as well as works like the famous altarpiece, the *Burial of the Count of Orgaz*. The *View of Toledo* is a rather strange interpretation, considering that this city in the very center of Spain would ordinarily be charged with sunlight—every form crystal-clear, and crisp. El Greco has characteristically chosen to show the city in an unusual aspect—during or just before a storm—and the ordinary color and space elements are deliberately altered for the artist's purposes. The inhospitable grayish-greens that suffuse the picture are just as "unreal" as the arbitrary rearrangement of buildings and the movement of the space upward instead of back into the picture.

For El Greco, this ancient place, inhabited at different times by Romans, Visigoths, Moors, Jews, and Christians, is not a city of joy and light; it is rather a symbol of doom and dark despair. On the right bank of the river in the lower part of the picture there are tiny wormlike creatures which seem to be human beings. But they are unimportant; it is the general emotional and mystical effect of this land that the painter wishes to convey.

Unquestionably these are all conscious techniques used to attain desired artistic ends, for El Greco was not a mad mystic. Indeed he was a very aggressive and often unspiritual person who did not hesitate to go to court over payment for a picture. This does not challenge the painter's sincerity, but it does away with explanations of his art that allege madness or bad eyesight. He was as aware of what he was doing as the painters of our own day who have found in him a constant source of inspiration. If El Greco's art appears somewhat strained and mannered, it is because he was a sixteenth-century individual responding to the pressures of his time.

27   EL GRECO   *View of the City of Toledo*

PIETER BRUEGHEL THE ELDER

PIETER BRUEGHEL was probably the most significant and exciting painter in northern Europe during the middle part of the sixteenth century. Carrying forward the sturdy simplicity and emotional strength of the great Dürer, this Flemish painter produced impressive commentaries on the events and people of his time, and the most important group of landscapes in centuries.

Born in the little Flemish town of Brueghel, the painter was drawn to the great commercial and artistic center of Antwerp. In that period Antwerp was what Bruges had been a century earlier, in the time of van Eyck and van der Weyden. Brueghel grew to manhood on the full tide of the great changes that were altering the character of Europe. Erasmus of Rotterdam had put his humanistic and skeptical mark on contemporary thought, and in Antwerp the great presses of the house of Plantin were busy printing the new ideas as fast as they appeared.

When, early in the sixteenth century, the Protestant Reformation came to the Spanish-owned Netherlands, the King of Spain sent his mercenaries to keep the Dutch and Flemings in order. In the attempt to cow the populace, the invading soldiers murdered, raped, and pillaged. This side of Flemish history was referred to in masked ways by Brueghel through canvases that supposedly showed generalized subjects like *The Massacre of the Innocents* or the *Triumph of Death*. Sometimes he used fanciful references such as the *Magpie on the Gallows*—a more openly defiant satire of the Spaniards and their free-swinging nooses.

Brueghel's professional career began with his apprenticeship at the age of twenty to a Pieter Coeck from whom he derived some of his feeling for the fantastic as well as his manual technique. Later he went with another master who was a picture dealer and print publisher, Jerome Cock. Upon his admission to the painter's guild in 1551, Brueghel went on the customary journey to gain experience. In spite of the wars of the time between Charles V of Spain, and the French king, Francis I, he got as far as Italy at the height of the fame of Michelangelo, Titian, and Tintoretto.

On his return to Antwerp he produced the humorous engravings and goblin pictures that earned him the name of Pieter the Droll. With a merchant friend he went among the peasants to fairs and marriages. Dressed in country style both men brought presents and were readily accepted by the merrymakers. These experiences were the basis of such pictures as the well-known *The Wedding Dance* (fig. 28) and similar scenes in which the simple people of Flanders are shown enjoying themselves. There can be no questioning of Brueghel's sympathy with these folk; there is none of the satire or condescension often met with in other peasant paintings. Strong, lusty figures are seen in the measures of a lively dance. No attempt is made to gloss over or to prettify the natural crudities of behavior.

Yet a picture of this type cannot be looked upon merely as an everyday folk or genre scene painted for the sake of quaint subject matter. In addition to showing his pleasure in this event and his feeling for the people, Brueghel has created a careful pattern of forms, colors, lines, and directional emphases. These make the individual human being part of a systematic decorative arrangement. In this sense the picture may be compared to the mannerist art of Holbein, or to some of the sixteenth-century Italians who reduce their characters to pictorial elements by telescoping space, distorting a form and repeating a color emphasis here and there. In this particular work, Brueghel has ar-

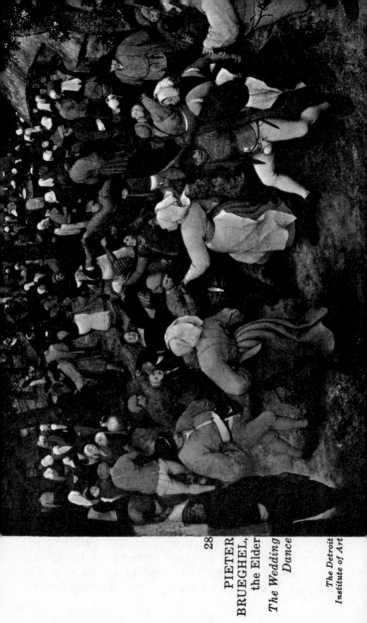

28

PIETER
BRUEGHEL,
the Elder
*The Wedding
Dance*

*The Detroit
Institute of Art*

29

PIETER
BRUEGHEL,
the Elder

*The Unfaithful
Shepherd*

*Courtesy of the
Johnson Collection,
Philadelphia*

ranged his people in a number of interwoven lines that move back and forth in curves through the lower part of the picture. This complex and tightly knit group is related to the rest of the painting through the repetition of accents of red, white, black, and yellow, resulting in an all-over pattern.

The figures themselves are often reduced to decorative outlines in which detail is held to a minimum in the interest of the over-all pattern. For the same reason individual emotions are not stressed. Instead, the entire turbulence of the dance and its total expressive quality is able to emerge. We may think of this picture as the essence of movement rather than the portrayal of a specific event, although the scene itself undoubtedly was witnessed by the painter. This is a modern viewpoint, but it is also a traditional aspect of painting as seen in Michelangelo's *Jeremiah* or El Greco's *View of Toledo* and countless others.

The Unfaithful Shepherd (fig. 29) illustrates Brueghel's interest in nature with its allegorical possibilities, and his equally strong feelings about contemporary events. This scene, in which a shepherd abandons his flock to the wolves, is probably a reference to an actual official—political or clerical—who ran away when conditions became difficult. As usual in Brueghel's scenes of this type, the meanness of mankind is contrasted to the beauty of nature, a beauty that remains constant in the face of tawdry but essentially transient behavior.

Brueghel's landscapes have a richness of mood and color, an atmospheric quality that carry us back to the earlier Flemish and foreshadow the paintings of later Netherlands artists. At the same time, the diagonal composition in which the main character rushes out of the picture at an angle and follows the twisting paths across the fields, is similar to the arrangements of the contemporary Tintoretto in Italy. The placing of a large object in the foreground, beyond which the rest of the picture is seen, is also an effect frequently used by the Italians.

This allegory shows Brueghel's own feeling for his land

and its people, in a time and place of strong emotion. The religious disturbances were climaxed in 1569 when Protestants fought Catholics and civilians fought soldiers. A few months before Brueghel's death, these events launched the eleven years of war that eventually freed part of the Netherlands from Spain.

GIOVANNI GUERCINO

SEVENTEENTH-CENTURY Europe saw the emergence of three powerful new forces that had an important effect on the art of the time. The first of these was an organized counterattack against the Protestant Reformation. The Catholic Church led by the militant new Society of Jesus developed a sweeping program of education and propaganda to stimulate the religious sentiment of the faithful and to win new adherents. Its activities were directly reflected in an architecture, sculpture, and painting that emphasized the pathetic, the melodramatic, and the profoundly emotional.

Secondly, there was a broader conception of the globe which resulted from an increasing knowledge of the non-European world, especially the Americas. In a startling reversal of the age-old idea that man was the center of the universe, the earth was now found to revolve about the sun. At the same time the world was thought of as larger and more complex than ever before. The effects of these new beliefs are seen in the use of smaller figures in landscapes and, more important, in the constant reference to an infinite rather than a limited space.

The third factor that distinguished this period was the solidification of monarchies, which gave painting in many lands a distinctly aristocratic aspect. This stabilization helped the development of the middle class which now emerged as a new patron of the arts.

In Catholic countries like Italy, Spain, Flanders, and France there developed a combination of the aristocratic

30 GUERCINO *Death of St. Petronilla*

and the emotional religious elements, as in Guercino, Rubens, and others. In middle-class countries like Holland the accent was on naturalistic qualities, although the idea of infinity remained a potent factor. These various traits appeared as different phases of the new Baroque style of the seventeenth century.

In the Academy of Bologna, the Carracci family and their prize pupil Giovanni Guercino proceeded on the assumption that all good things had already been accomplished. It was their expressed intention to imitate and combine the achievements of various masters. In their art one can recognize the drawing of Michelangelo, the light and dark effects of Leonardo, the sentiment of Raphael. The form and composition of the late Renaissance had been turned into a formula. Yet there are some features far removed from the well-balanced and serene works of the High Renaissance.

Guercino's melodramatic *Death of St. Petronilla* (fig. 30) shows the saint being lowered into her grave by two straining men who bend over her in a kind of arc. At angles, from left and right, groups of spectators come into the picture; one group expresses the pathos of the scene, the other a sort of shocked curiosity. Their outward movement is matched by a similarly flaring arrangement above where Christ and His angels come in from the left to greet the spirit of the saint arriving on a cloud. Overhead an angel bears the martyr's crown. Together the four groups form a diamond shape. Each unit of the four has some element of deliberate incompleteness about it, as though the painter wanted us to go further—out of the picture and off into space. This same quality also lends an air of excitement, whereas in the paintings of the High Renaissance both form and mood are always self-contained. Earlier pictures move to a single point of focus, as the *Last Supper* of Leonardo or *The Creation of Adam* by Michelangelo. Here the composition is much more diffuse; all the groups revolve about an open space in the center from which the light seems to come.

The individuals, though based on everyday types, have a generalized appearance which comes from the use of earlier forms. In the sky above, the Christ is a dignified and elegant figure, as is the soul of the saint herself. It seems, then, that a certain number of borrowed ideas have been adapted to the contemporary need for religious inspiration and stimulation.

A much more dramatic example of Guercino's ability to project forms into space may be seen in the *Aurora* (fig. 31) of the Villa Ludovisi in Rome. This is a simple classical theme: the goddess of the dawn rides through the sky in her chariot, strewing flowers behind her toward her husband Tithonus. The dynamic movement of the horses and the flying birds surges forward into the light of day. Guercino has painted a series of remarkably foreshortened pilasters on the walls and the vaulted ceiling overhead, representing the outside of the Villa; he has also shown the rocky landscape around it. Into this environment, riding through the air on clouds, Aurora's chariot sweeps triumphantly across the sky. Light already coming from the left brightens the tops of the supporting clouds, while the rest of the light is still to come as the day advances. Here, as in the movement itself, is a feeling of things about to happen. Here too is a sense of the dynamic, the constant motion that is an essential quality of Baroque art.

Even though the painting looks like a complete work, it is part of a longer and more extensive composition with Night at one end and Day at the other. Similar to some Venetian ceiling decorations of the Renaissance, the entire work is designed to be seen from one fixed point of view, directly below the main entrance to the room. The various sections revolve visually about this fixed point like planets about a sun. Each portion is as important as every other in the total effect. Their relationship is like that of a universe where all stars are effective and vital, where all travel through infinite space.

31 GUERCINO *Aurora*

Villa Ludovisi, Rome (Alinari)

MICHELANGELO MERISI
DA CARAVAGGIO

FEW artists in history have exerted as extraordinary an influence as the tempestuous and short-lived Caravaggio. He was destined to turn a large part of European art away from the ideal viewpoint of the Renaissance to the concept that simple reality was of primary importance. The difference lies between what an artist thinks is the *proper* way to show something, and what he actually sees. Thus Caravaggio represented a separate Baroque attitude different from the still idealizing Guercino and his fellow academicians.

Born Michelangelo Merisi in the little town of Caravaggio which gave him his name, he started his working career as a plaster mixer for some fresco painters. He soon began to imitate them and, after a number of years of portrait, fruit, and flower painting, visited Venice and then Rome. He learned from the artists of both cities and attracted attention with his extraordinary realism. In the Rome of that day, the paintings of Guercino had represented the norm—complicated religious and classical allegories in the ennobling technique of the Renaissance—and so we may realize what the impact of Caravaggio must have been.

A picture like the *Boy Bitten by a Lizard* (fig. 32) brings together the monumentality of the older art (which earned for Caravaggio the title of "the last classicist") and a new method of seeing and painting that is his own contribution. Instead of idealizing the form, Caravaggio is much more concerned with what an object really looks like. He shows the simple natural act of a boy whose finger has been caught by the little lizard—a straightforward and un-ideal conception. Moreover he also shows that a picture need not have a good-looking or classical subject. This type of treatment had been restricted to a tortured saint, but with Caravaggio it could be used for any theme.

His interest in the specific quality of objects and substances may be seen in the careful and precise rendering of the water bottle with its flower, the cherries, or the hair of the boy. These are all done in a limpid and clear light, with a regard for their materiality that anticipates seventeenth-century artists like Vermeer or nineteenth-century painters' like Manet. Most important is the fact that these naturalistic effects are shown for their own sake, for the sake of painting itself, and not for the purpose of stimulating sorrow for a martyr or some other exalted sentiment.

Caravaggio's interest in simple everyday people was later extended into many other fields. Scenes such as his various *Card Players* present the atmosphere of the inns he often frequented. This development brought with it a more dramatic handling of light which he was also able to apply to religious subjects. His *The Death of the Virgin* (fig. 33) is a typical Caravaggio treatment of a religious theme. Instead of dignified and glorified personages, a group of simple everyday people is gathered about the funeral couch. Nor is the Virgin Herself more than an ordinary woman, except for the lightly indicated halo.

With dramatic intent, the painter has caused the light to be thrown across these figures as though from a spotlight. This theatrical device controls the illumination as it moves across the heads at the upper left down to the right where it brightens the face of the main character, the dead Virgin. With clever planning, the faces about Her are either in partial shadow or bent so that their features do not distract from the artist's main purpose. Nevertheless this is a descriptive light the main function of which seems to be the creation of form in the picture space. In spite of Caravag-

32 CARAVAGGIO *Boy Bitten by a Lizard*

gio's avowed dislike of the conventional art of his period, he cannot help being a part of the expression of the time in his own way. The whole idea of evoking sympathy for the dead Virgin conveys this, as does the diagonal composition. Moreover, as in most Baroque paintings, there is a deliberate incompleteness; cut-off figures carry the eye out of the painting on all sides, and back into it as well.

Many people of that day were much offended by this "vulgarization" of religious art, by the abandonment of religious nobility in favor of a realism which demanded that the artist paint only what he could see. Caravaggio tied wings on the backs of his models when he had to paint angels; later, Courbet in the ninetenth century would refuse to paint angels at all because he could not see them.

In addition to these revolutionary religious treatments, Caravaggio managed to get himself into trouble in various other ways. A hot-tempered individual, he was "quick on the draw" and wielded dagger and sword with deadly efficiency. On several occasions he was forced to leave town just one step ahead of the police; but due to the highly placed patronage that he enjoyed, he was recalled to Rome. In Naples, where he went until things cooled off, he found himself among the toughest bunch of artists and cutthroats of the period; but he managed to hold his own.

His adventures in Malta, where he went in search of a decoration (the Cross of Malta), resulted in a term of imprisonment and a spectacular escape. Back in Naples, he took ship for Rome but was stopped by Spanish officers who thought he was a criminal they were looking for. By the time they cleared him, the ship had sailed, and he was left at an obscure point on the coast where, without food or baggage, he caught a fever and died.

The effect of Caravaggio's two styles, the clear limpid naturalistic early manner and the more spectacular light and dark realism of his later works, is seen throughout the seventeenth and following centuries.

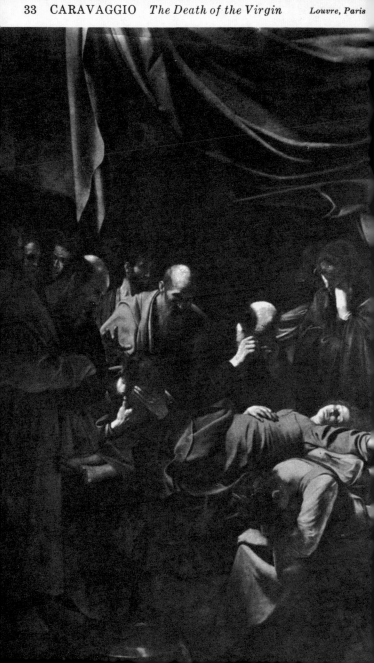

PETER PAUL RUBENS

AMONG the courtly artists of seventeenth-century Baroque painting, no one was so exciting or so influential as Peter Paul Rubens. He was a product of the royalist and Catholic environment of Flanders which had remained part of the Spanish empire. His works present a brilliantly effective mixture of the chief trends of the day.

Rubens was the son of a minor official at the court of William of Orange. He was brought up in Antwerp in the relatively calm atmosphere following the Treaty of Utrecht which divided the Netherlands into Catholic Flanders and Protestant Holland. Since his artistic education was begun under local artists who had been adapting Italian styles, Rubens was well prepared for his early stay in Italy under the protection of the Duke of Mantua. In Italy he naturally came into contact with all the aspects of the High Renaissance and early Baroque. He bought one of Caravaggio's pictures and copied another. He also did sketches after Leonardo and Tintoretto, as well as studies that suggest Titian and other masters.

Rubens returned to Antwerp in 1609 to become court painter to the Spanish viceroy, Archduke Ferdinand. His studio became the artistic center of Flanders. Many already established men worked for him in the immense picture "factory" that was set up to cope with the flood of orders. Some were set to painting animals, others landscape background, and others did still life. The master furnished the basic design and united all the elements by his own finishing touches.

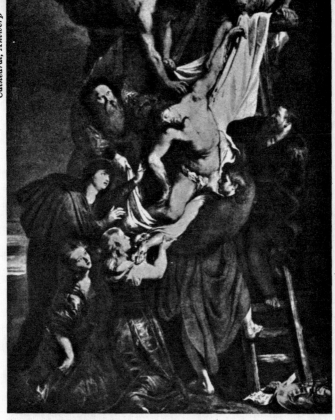

34 RUBENS *The Descent from the Cross*

One of the earliest and in some ways most typical of Rubens' adaptations of past traditions is his famous *The Descent from the Cross* (fig. 34). Here the borrowings from Italy have been thoroughly digested and converted into a personal expression at once pathetic and impressive, aristocratic and naturalistic, worldly and religious. Basically, it offers a rectangular design through which a curved diagonal from upper right to lower left carries the body of the Savior on a white cloth. A dramatic light cuts through this area, highlighting the moment. At the corners, the figures flare out into space and take the action beyond the immediate scope of the picture. The light suggests the melodramatic realism of Caravaggio; the swelling muscles of the Christ and the man leaning down from the upper left suggest Michelangelo. Mary Magdalene and her companion at the lower left show the aristocratic side of this art, for they are ladies of the court rather than poor friends and relatives of the Savior.

All these elements: the pathetic, the aristocratic, and even the sensuous, combine to make Rubens the characteristic painter of the courtly Baroque style, and the most popular as well. Pictures like *The Descent from the Cross* sum up the basic feeling of the Catholic counter-Reformation. They fulfill the desire for a dramatic expression of revealed truth in which the spectator is directly involved both psychologically and physically. Churches and private patrons, kings and commoners wanted these paintings, both for their religious qualities and for their sheer magnificence.

Among the most important commissions received by Rubens was a series of paintings for Marie de Médicis, the Queen of France. These pictures are now in the Louvre, but they were originally designed for her private palace, the Luxembourg, where they remained for many years. The various scenes tell in rich and splendid allegory the story of the lady's life. At that time they had the important effect of spreading the Flemish Baroque style into France. Later, throughout the eighteenth century, French painters came

35

RUBENS

*The Judgment
of Paris*

to the Luxembourg to study them, as earlier Italian artists had gone to the Brancacci Chapel in Florence to study the frescoes of Masaccio.

Rubens' genius as a composer in light and dark, in backward and forward movement is also expressed in a variety of other subjects. These include probing portraits of the royal family, friends, and others, landscapes, classical stories and hunting pictures. The rich exuberance of his style is perhaps best illustrated in classical themes such as *The Judgment of Paris* (fig. 35). Here a remarkably vivid and sensuous pagan feeling is conveyed by the cultured Rubens' interpretation of ancient legend. There is little regard for archaeological fact in pictures of this kind; they are studies of the nude out of doors, rather than careful reconstructions of antique stories. Most of them are based on studies he made of his charming young second wife, Helene Fourment. Here these have been woven into a subtly modulated fabric of textures and surface movements. The forms become part of a twinkling all-over design that relates the three nudes to the wonderfully transparent landscape background.

In the course of many diplomatic journeys on behalf of the Spanish government, Rubens visited Madrid in 1628. There he made friends with the great painter Velásquez whom he influenced. In Madrid he also studied the rich Titian collection whose effect is felt in the glowing *Judgment of Paris*. Other missions during the following year took him to England where he decorated a ceiling in Whitehall Palace for King Charles.

Rubens remains one of the truly extraordinary figures in the history of painting: artist, diplomat, man of letters, and collector of art. His is the sole credit for creating the northern Baroque style. Later artists refer to him again and again, from Watteau to Delacroix, and even down to our own day.

DIEGO VELÁSQUEZ

VELÁSQUEZ is one of the outstanding masters of visual painting in modern times. Like some other masters of the seventeenth century, notably Caravaggio, Le Nain, Vermeer, and Frans Hals, he was dedicated to painting what was clearly visible to the eye. Contrary to the Renaissance method, he portrayed what he actually saw rather than what he wanted to find.

Born in Seville, of noble family, his full name was Diego Rodriguez de Silva y Velásquez. He went to Madrid in 1622, and soon was made court painter, at a salary barely sufficient for him and his family. But there was the privilege of being in constant attendance on King Philip IV, wearing his cast-off clothing, painting his portrait, and those of the queen, the royal children, and other shining lights of the seventeenth-century Spanish court. Philip IV, one of the most painted monarchs in history, had a passageway constructed from his own apartments to the studio of the artist and would arrive at odd hours to watch him at work or to be painted once more. Working in a sort of gold-fish bowl, Velásquez' situation is characteristic of the "protective custody" which surrounded many official painters of the period.

His early works were probably done in Seville under his teachers, Herrera and Pacheco. These paintings show a clear relationship to the everyday subjects and lighting of Caravaggio who was already known in Spain. From the very beginning Velásquez was interested in atmosphere, still-life, reflections in mirrors, and similar effects.

36 VELÁSQUEZ *Portrait of Philip IV of Spain*

When he became court painter in 1623, he was expected to paint court portraits, make trips to buy pictures, plan celebrations for the royal family, and help establish an academy of art. As an employee of the royal family, the portraits he painted have a peculiar quality. He could not show his employers as they really were—neither physically attractive nor especially bright. Nor did his sense of realism allow him to indulge in the glorification and flattery that run through the portraits of Titian and his followers. Thus these official portrayals by Velásquez take on a kind of objectivity. Although by no means openly condemnatory, they imply in the very lack of feeling that there is something wrong.

The *Portrait of Philip IV of Spain* (fig. 36), shows a somewhat monumentalized outline of a dignified gentleman in Spanish black relieved only by the gold chain and white collar and cuffs. A not especially attractive red in the hair, the muddy complexion, the outthrust Hapsburg jaw and pendulous lower lip are present but not too overtly. Velásquez has avoided a definite judgment, giving an evaluation that is neither one thing nor another.

He has concerned himself with catching the light as it comes out around the edges of a flat, two-dimensional form. In other words, he is occupied with seeing the figure and catching an instantaneous visual image, rather than with a drawn-out interpretation of character. It is as though, having just come into the room with its subdued light, we see a man for the first time. We try to identify him by looking attentively at the face, while the form in its black dress remains somewhat obscure and out of focus. Thus the face and the hands are roundly modeled, but the form remains flat, as it often does at first glance—the only glance which the painter allows us.

If Philip's body lacks substance, it is because of this rapid visual impression which the painter wishes to give. A final consideration on the technical side: most of the picture was painted without the sitter's presence. Only the head was done from life; the costume was sent along later to be filled in. Whatever the reasons, this style links Velásquez to the future—to that other Spaniard Goya, in the late eighteenth century and to Manet in nineteenth-century France. He becomes part of the Realist-Impressionist tradition that is so important in the modern history of art.

One of the most brilliant visual effects is the famous *The Maids of Honor* (fig. 37) painted toward the end of his life. In the foreground is the little Infanta Margareta surrounded by her maids-in-waiting, dwarfs, dogs, and servants. Before an enormous easel the painter may be seen working on some sort of picture involving the little princess. Looking past these people through the atmosphere-filled room, we see a rear starcase where an equerry has paused to witness the scene. He and the group in the foreground are watching the king and queen who have come to observe their daughter being painted. The royal pair is reflected in a small mirror hanging on the wall. In order to make this reality convincing, Velásquez has employed subtle gradations of color and atmosphere. The young ladies in the foreground are strongest in color and sharpest in focus; the man on the staircase is seen less clearly and the royal pair reflected in the mirror is visually the furthest away and the least clearly seen.

Although the life of Velásquez was filled with rather routine tasks, it was considerably enlivened by such feats of ingenuity as *The Maids of Honor*. The achievement may not have been fully appreciated by his patrons, but it was the result of a conscious aesthetic effort on his part. Rubens' visit in 1628, his own trip to Italy on Rubens' advice, and a second trip later to buy pictures for the king were the highlights in a life dedicated to royal service. When he died in 1660, he was about three thousand dollars in debt to the royal treasury.

37   VELÁSQUEZ   *The Maids of Honor*

NICOLAS POUSSIN

In what the French themselves call the Great Century, the painting of Poussin stands out for its tremendous clarity and logic, its controlled emotions. Poussin represents the official and classical side of French art, the more logical and well-balanced aspect which appears also in the rational philosophy and theater of the time. His is a picture of an earlier world, the antiquity of Rome or of early Christianity. Most of his paintings evoke this long-lost and somewhat romantically viewed period of dignity and quiet.

Born in Les Andelys, Poussin studied in Amiens and went to Paris when he was eighteen. There he became friendly with an Italian poet, the Cavaliere Marino, who became his patron. The only important work he did in the dozen years he spent in Paris was to help in the decorative work on the Luxembourg Palace which was being prepared for the magnificent series of Rubens pictures. Whatever contact there may have been between the two men, the robust power of the Flemish artist never touched the sober and serious vein of the French painter.

In 1624 Poussin left for Rome where he worked for Cardinal Barberini and made a number of drawings from ancient sculpture remains for the antiquarian Cassiano del Pozzo. He was naturally affected by the great masters of the Renaissance as well as by the literature of ancient times and the writings of Dürer on technical subjects. Poussin tried to bring these various influences together, to find the rational basis of each style, and to discover how it could contribute to the combination he wished to achieve. Thus he was able to understand the formal logic behind the compositions of Raphael and at the same time to appreciate the rich sensuous qualities of Titian; occasionally he would unite the two in his search for the perfect synthesis of the great traditions.

In *The Triumph of Flora* (fig. 38), the sweeping patterns and rhythms of people and landscape move from right to left across the picture. Long undulating curves carry a dignified but effective motion. Up-and-down movements from the right are balanced by down-and-up movements from the left, bringing the side-to-side activity into dynamic balance. The many forms placed in the foreground and the gradual recession of trees and hills give a similar balance to the front-to-back movement. Further logic may be seen in the way the figures are paired and paralleled, especially the man and woman in the lower left and the joined legs of the three people at the right.

What is most striking is that the sense of physical well-being suggests Titian, while the actual physical shapes are reminiscent of Raphael (fig. 17). Yet the combination is characteristically Poussin. The logic of the seventeenth century dominates in the arrangement and control of the forms, in the careful balance of the spatial elements.

The richness, splendor, and sense of continuous motion mark this as a Baroque expression. But the difference between Poussin's art and the more tumultuous and melodramatic efforts of many Italian contemporaries may be seen by referring to Guercino's *Aurora* (fig. 31), a very similar theme. In comparison with the visual excitement and plunging motion of the Italian picture, Poussin's work is a model of precise and cautious composition.

Poussin was recalled to Paris in 1640 as "first painter to the king." His actual job was to supervise the decorations in the Louvre Palace, the king's official residence. After a frustrating two years during which local Parisian artists undercut him at every opportunity, Poussin went back to Rome in 1642 and spent the rest of his life there. At this

38 POUSSIN *The Triumph of Flora*

Louvre, Paris (Alinari)

39 POUSSIN *Orpheus and Eurydice*

point the painter turned in upon himself. He took refuge in the spirit of the ancient world which he found so potent in the city of Rome. From this period date such pictures as the *Orpheus and Eurydice* (fig. 39) with their self-conscious and delicate evocation of things past. It is a simple, quiet world that the painter portrays here. In a typical arrangement the "actors" are placed in the center foreground with carefully balanced elements on either side, and a large open space between the downstage area and the background.

Poussin tells a story of ancient times—*Orpheus and Eurydice*, the *Burial of Phocion*, or *Landscape with St. Matthew*—but the story itself is the least important part of the picture, for one looks much like another. The vital feature is the feeling of distance that lies between the spectator and the past which is symbolized by the Roman buildings in the background. We can only look at this past; we cannot touch it, since between foreground and background there is usually either a body of water or some other area just as difficult to cross. This then is Poussin's personal poetry. The deliberate psychological and visual separation is also used by later painters such as Corot, and by others in our own day.

An equally important and influential factor is the careful way in which the painter carries the eye into the picture. He makes the spatial transitions with smaller blocklike geometric forms. These follow each other inward to the rear and then come forward again. They are reminiscent of similar landscapes constructed by Cézanne, the great rational painter of the late nineteenth century.

Although the Paris of his day apparently rejected him, Poussin remains in many ways the most typical French painter of his century.

LOUIS LE NAIN

THE growing importance of the merchant group in sevententh-century France went hand in hand with the centralization of that country under the powerful monarchy. Both developed at the expense of the increasingly impoverished feudal lords. During this period the merchants began to figure in the culture of the time through a new realism found in the work of such artists as Georges de la Tour, and the three Le Nain brothers: Antoine, Mathieu, and Louis. They represent the more naturalistic and middle class phase of seventeenth-century French painting, quite different from that of Poussin.

The work of the Le Nains, especially Louis, revives the unpretentious simplicity and naturalism of the earlier northern style, that of the fifteenth-century Flemish and German masters. The collaboration of the three brothers makes it rather difficult to separate their techniques, but, apparently, Antoine was the most provincial and even primitive, Mathieu the most elegant in his imitation of Dutch works, and Louis the most powerful and interesting. Because of Louis' monumental figures, his sensitive glowing color, his three-dimensional form, and his tremendous feeling for the subjects portrayed, he emerges as one of the most significant leaders of his time.

While Poussin represents the rational, balanced, and controlled upper-class art of the French Academy and its ideals, Louis Le Nain indicates a turning toward a less pretentious and less intellectual interpretation, one in which atmosphere and mood dominate. Although born in the provincial town of Laon the Le Nains were as important as the more sophisticated artists. In Paris they painted *genre*, or everyday pictures; nevertheless they were admitted as founding members of the French Academy. But because they remained outside the main tradition, the pompous "grand manner" so favored by the deep thinkers of their day, their influence remained slight until the modern revival of realistic art.

The Caravaggio tradition of dramatic lighting effects and simple, unassuming people may be seen in such works of Louis Le Nain as *The Forge* (fig. 40). Rather than the broad luminous color areas of the Italian master, the general color quality tends toward a silvery-gray tonality. Even more important, the character of the figures is different. Le Nain was a pioneer, for his people were, perhaps, the first representations of real workers in the history of painting.

Caravaggio, even in everyday scenes, dealt with tavern subjects—fortunetellers, card players, and gypsies; his characters, although poor, differ in nature from Le Nain's simple folk who work in a blacksmith shop. To be sure, other painters in the seventeenth century, especially the Dutch, pictured farmers or workmen drinking and having a good time. But their emphasis was on a humorous condescension that must have made their middle-class Dutch customers feel superior. Le Nain, on the other hand, shows a seriousness akin to the solemnity of earlier northern painters. He magnifies the importance of the individual worker or peasant, and invests them with a solemn grandeur. To this extent Louis Le Nain is perhaps as humanistic as any Renaissance master. He may also be compared with certain nineteenth-century European painters and writers who dwelt on the dignity of labor and surrounded it with an aura of nobility, like Millet in *The Gleaners*, or George Eliot in *Silas Marner*.

In *The Forge*, the statue-like quality of the individuals results from the light which, falling upon them from the fire, models their forms in the dimness of the room.

40 LE NAIN *The Forge*   *Louvre, Paris*

Though separated from each other in a simple, clear way, they are nevertheless combined in a powerful arc that stretches across the painting. This power is accented by the curious immobility of the actors who turn as if to consider the observer, to give him "Good day" in the traditional slow manner of the country.

The universal nature of Le Nain characters might be compared with those of Brueghel who was equally sympathetic in his way. The figures of the Flemish master, however, tend to be subordinated to a flat pattern and so have less importance. In Le Nain's art, the people acquire an individual importance; each is set apart in his own envelope of atmosphere and his own solemn thoughts, as in a religious painting.

Another instance of this seriousness is the *Peasants' Meal* (fig. 41) which shows once more the provincial painter in the big city. He is interested in the same plastic truth as before, and his serious feeling about people and objects leaves the actors immobile and isolated, in their respective thoughts. Here again is the loving treatment of small objects of everyday use, the slow arching rhythm of the heads from one side to the other, the feeling of a life foreign to the bustle of the big city.

These people are having a meal, but they raise their glasses or taste the wine as though it were a sacrament of some kind. The little boy in the rear holds a violin in his hands and gazes down at it with rapt absorption. These are simple persons, yet they have a dignity and sense of worth that is deep and genuine. It is not accidental that French writers in our day have turned to Louis Le Nain and his peasants as examples of the most humanistic expression of their national tradition.

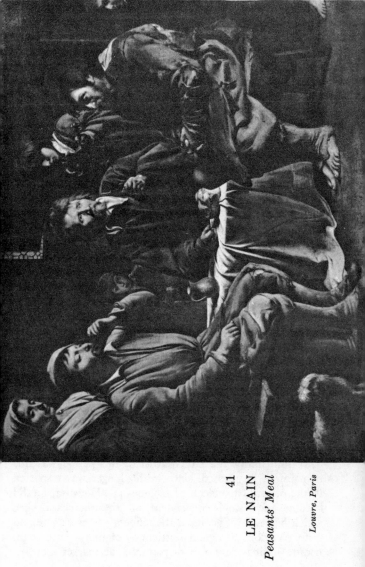

41

LE NAIN
Peasants' Meal

Louvre, Paris

JAN VERMEER

THE Holland of Jan Vermeer was different in many ways from other European countries of the seventeenth century. Because it had been able to break away from Spain during the sixteenth-century religious wars, Holland was neither Catholic nor royalist. It had become a conservative, middle class, Protestant democracy. The artist, like any other businessman, was part of the system of free competition. There was no longer an organized church to give him commissions—religious art was actually frowned upon—nor was there the important patronage of a court aristocracy.

As a result, the average Dutch painter turned from religious scenes to an art concerned primarily with the everyday world; from an art of elegance to an expression of middle class seriousness. His feeling for the spiritual was now channeled into converting the commonplace into something more significant, as in the painting of Jan Vermeer. Conversely, spiritual ideas and emotions tended to be brought down to a more mundane level, as in Rembrandt. Both viewpoints were, in fact, part of the two-hundred-year-old heritage from Jan van Eyck.

Within limits, the Dutch artist of this period was free to paint as he pleased, since he no longer was restricted to the prescribed subjects of religious art. However, he did become increasingly dependent on the merchant class which had not yet acquired the refinements of culture and taste. Without the guild restrictions of monarchist countries to limit the number of painters, the market soon be-

42   VERMEER   *Officer and Laughing Girl*

came as saturated with artists and pictures as it is today. In order to compete, the painter had to produce what his new customers demanded—pictures that were clearly drawn, richly colored and which glorified in different ways the wealthy burghers, their families, and their highly valued material possessions. But even this did not always guarantee a livelihood. Frans Hals died in the poorhouse; Rembrandt, losing his popularity, ended bankrupt; and Vermeer, whose pictures certainly were popular, had much financial trouble.

Jan Vermeer offers the most impressive reflection of the worldly side of seventeenth-century Dutch life—its love of fine furniture, attractive women, and lavish clothing. Like Le Nain, though on a more cosmopolitan level, he glorifies commonplace objects and gives them an importance which, in another culture, would be reserved for classical or holy scenes. The *Officer and Laughing Girl* (fig. 42) may recall the sanctity of two haloed figures confronting each other in an interior, but now they are having a chat and a drink. This simple, even trivial activity is raised to a higher level by the rich warm atmosphere that suffuses the room, the clear glowing colors in which the characters are dressed, their great dignity and self-confidence, and the way in which the various parts of the picture are brought together.

The atmospheric quality had been used long ago by van Eyck; it becomes important again in the Baroque art of this period. That is just one of the glorifying elements here. Even more striking is the "touchable" quality that we get from the objects in the room—table, chairs, glass, cloth, map rods, and window panes. Under the enamel-like surface each substance is realized with a crystal clarity that also recalls the interiors of the early northern masters. The strong composition is not only a formal element, it also serves to give strength and emphasis to what is happening. This is accomplished by the use of a clear silhouette for each form. Strong parallel curves are bound together in an arc which sweeps from the left-hand to the right-hand chair. The spectator is led from the boldly outlined soldier

43   VERMEER   *Young Woman with a Water Jug*

to the related curves of the smiling woman. The eye is aided by the lines of the table and the way the heads touch the window and the wall map. There is a constant moving pattern throughout, a kind of wheel arrangement with the forms revolving about an empty space in the center, as in other Baroque compositions.

Vermeer's relationship to the art of his period is also seen in the positive evocation of both distance and infinity. Through the open window daylight comes, connecting outside and inside in a space-creating fashion. Geographical distance is implied by the typical wall map, symbol of the great Dutch trading nation with colonies in Asia and America—far-off places which offered prosperity and success, places which were in everyone's mind.

Another instance of Baroque qualities is found in the *Young Woman with a Water Jug* (fig. 43). The strong feeling for the texture of substances and the almost religious seriousness mark this as a typical Vermeer work. The young girl is at the center of the wheel arrangement, lost in thought as she gazes through the window. As in most Vermeer pictures, light is the dominating factor. Here it is used to silhouette the young woman against the wall and to throw reflections from the blue window pane onto her face and white starched collar and hood. These reflections are almost Impressionist in their awareness of the influence of adjacent objects on each other. The blue cushion is mirrored in the silver bowl, and the figured tablecloth is reflected on the underside of the bowl.

Vermeer's life remains a mystery. It is known that he had a large family which apparently kept him scurrying for money. Once he had to borrow, at another time he endorsed a note for someone. Though his paintings brought good prices there were occasions when he had to trade pictures for food. Once a visitor to his studio related that he had absolutely nothing to sell but that he lived very well, even luxuriously. But none of this seems to have been permanent and the total result was the financial instability which became increasingly familiar to the "free artist" of the period. For two centuries after his death Vermeer was almost completely forgotten. Dealers sold his pictures as the work of the lesser Dutch genre painters. Today only thirty-seven priceless examples of his work remain extant.

REMBRANDT VAN RIJN

Rembrandt's story as artist and as human being can be understood only in the context of the new conventional Dutch middle class and their showy, though restricted tastes. He is the most spiritual emanation of an unspiritual age. In him the things of the soul are united with a mundane and humanitarian outlook that makes his art unique. Whereas Vermeer gives his middle class characters an elegant and impressive appearance, Rembrandt heightens the qualities of the spirit, yet brings these close to the interests of the ordinary man. In a period of intense materialism, his art is a reminder of other values, a symbol of the conscience of mankind.

The son of a Leyden miller, he absorbed a simplicity and strength from family readings of the Testaments. He attended Latin school and entered the university, but he had no taste for learning. Finally he was apprenticed to a local painter whose chief distinction was that he had been to Italy. After six months with a second teacher, Rembrandt left to work on his own. By the age of twenty-one he had begun to attract followers, and he left for Amsterdam, launched on a professional career as a portrait painter. This early manner, dignified, detailed and clear, guaranteed his popularity. Painting pictures of the well-to-do was the chief way for an artist to make a living in those days and Rembrandt did exceptionally well. He married Saskia van Uylenborch, bought a beautiful home, and furnished it lavishly.

44

REMBRANDT
*Pilate Washing
His Hands*

Courtesy of The
Metropolitan
Museum of Art,
New York

The death of his wife in 1642 and the poor response to the innovations of his *Night Watch* combined to turn the worldly Rembrandt away from the mainstream of Dutch art. He had been moving in a new direction even before this; the *Night Watch* itself was a climax. It was an attempt to add dramatic meaning to the group portrait of a company of civic guards. Unfortunately these people were accustomed to being painted in photographic fashion with everything clear-cut and straightforward. They were surprised at this mysteriously glowing picture in which some persons could be seen plainly, while others were bathed in a shadowy light.

Although he arose out of the middle class tradition, Rembrandt now cut himself off from it. He developed a subjective art featuring Biblical and classical subjects with their great human and spiritual possibilities. His painting became increasingly expressive rather than precise and descriptive. This fact made him less acceptable as an artist, while his unblessed relationship with his housekeeper Hendrickje Stoeffels made him less presentable socially. But Rembrandt remained an important factor in the art of Holland and influenced many others in his direction. In spite of his bankruptcy in 1657, he continued to paint prodigiously and even received occasional official commissions like the *Syndics of the Cloth Guild*. He lived now in an obscure quarter on the outskirts of the city. The fine house had been sold; his library of etchings and drawings disposed of—"collected by Rembrandt himself with much love and care," said the auctioneer's catalogue. But the paintings of the latter part of his life show no outward signs of the material impoverishment and physical disintegration of the man. Done with a marvelous subtlety of glowing golden-toned color they are wholly concerned with analyzing and projecting the state of the soul.

The *Self-Portrait* (color plate VII), like Rembrandt's many estimates of himself in etching, drawing, and painting, is a generalized rather than photographic work. Everything is subordinated to the interpretation of character.

Details are omitted in the form itself; it barely emerges from the background, because of the dark underpainting and the way in which the light is held within the picture. Only the face is luminous. Thus Rembrandt represents the climax of the Caravaggio tradition of spotlighting the area to which the painter wishes to call attention.

Rembrandt, however, was no longer interested in the kind of melodramatic picture he had done earlier. What is important is the meaningful probing glance of the eyes, directed toward and beyond us as the artist looks off into infinite space and his form melts into unknown space behind him. Although the painter here displays general Baroque techniques, he is not trying to arouse pity or fear through the violent projection of a three-dimensional figure or through agonies of body and lighting. All of Rembrandt's pictures in this culmination of his career poses a psychological or a philosophical problem. Here he presents an aging individual whose circumstances have changed markedly and who yet is able to think about life with neither self-pity nor despair.

For Rembrandt, the Bible was a living thing from which the lessons of life could be learned. In the *Pilate Washing His Hands* (fig. 44), done a few years before the painter's death, he poses the ever-present problem of social responsibility. His interpretation of this moment reveals the profundity of his insight. A life is at stake—but so is the position of the man to whom the people appeal for judgment and to whom the mob outside howls for blood.

Pilate is a tired, cynical old gentleman whose shadowed face exposes the sharp nose and chin, and the tight lips. He symbolically washes his hands of the whole matter. It would be risky to involve himself here, and he will have none of it. Behind him stands an old man symbolizing age and experience; before him is the youthful figure of innocence who pours the water. The lad's hands and body tie the man who turns his back on responsibility to the brutal mob lusting for its victim.

A sweeping arc, moving from the lower left up and

around to the lower right, is set off against the rectangular building and the opening beyond. Light now comes not from any perceptible source, as in ordinary Baroque painting, but from little pinpoints of light within the glowing rich and darker mass of the figures themselves. It is not a real, but rather a spiritual radiance which illumines his characters with a unique and universal meaning. It endures as a symbol of his profound feeling for mankind.

JEAN ANTOINE WATTEAU

FRENCH eighteenth-century art has become a byword for elegant and charming upper class paintings, gracefully curved and inlaid furniture, delicate shell-work, and intricate paneling. It stands in sharp contrast to the dignified and logical art of the seventeenth century as represented by Poussin. The era after Louis XIV is also important for the increasing number of pictures filled with middle class sentiment. In the conflict between these two major social forces the aristocratic gradually gave way to the bourgeois as the latter became powerful economically and politically. The merchant class in the previous century had been a force behind the scenes, lending financial support to the rising monarchy. Now it emerged an open and avowed opponent of the monarchy, demanding and ultimately getting its own place in the sun.

Antoine Watteau is the outstanding and most sensitive representative of the ideals and aims of the then still important French court. His ultracharming and delicate scenes of loving-making, of performances in the theater, of would-be classical subjects, must not be taken as actual portrayals of life among the upper classes. They are rather the ideals of that social group: its illusions of worldly and unworldly beauty, its aspirations, its feelings about love.

Born in Valenciennes near the Flemish border, some forty years after the death of Rubens, Watteau absorbed much from the seventeenth-century master. His work displays the firm flesh and pink skin of the Rubens women as

45 WATTEAU *Jupiter and Antiope*

46 WATTEAU *The Embarkation for the Isle of Cythera*

well as the silky textures of their suave costumes. In both technique and spirit, Watteau continued the rich sensuous elegance of the northern Baroque style, though tempered by the graceful and more delicate imagery of the new age.

He came to Paris for the first time in 1712, studied with some rather mediocre teachers, and worked in an art factory turning out devotional pictures on a "conveyor belt" system. Each artist added his particular touch to the paintings which were produced in wholesale quantities. For three francs a week and meagre food, Watteau contributed countless figures of St. Nicholas. From there he went to the studio of Claude Gillot where he acquired a taste for the increasingly popular pictures of the theater and very soon excelled his master. Jealousy led to a quarrel and Watteau left to enter the shop to Claude Audran, custodian of the Luxembourg Palace where Rubens executed his famous series on the life of Marie de Médicis a hundred years before.

The differences and similarities between Watteau and Rubens may be seen in the *Jupiter and Antiope* (fig. 45). Its sensuous handling of the vibrantly colored nude, its building up of forms with touches of color rather than contour lines, and its sweeping circular composition are all Rubens. But the elongation and grace of the body, the small and delicate shape of the head are elements of the new and less grandiose manner that developed after the severe logic-dominated Louis XIV period. This charming and gracious style, heir to the richness and elegance of the aristocratic phase of Baroque art, is known as the Rococo.

A few years after Watteau's arrival in Paris, the long suppressed Italian companies of strolling players, the *Commedia dell'arte*, were permitted to resume their performances. These plays, together with the French theater itself, furnished Watteau with many useful themes. In them were reflected the unending quest for gaiety and diversion, as well as the artificial code of manners prescribed for the art of love-making by the elegant courtiers. For Watteau personally, the lavish theatrical displays and even the idea of love itself was touched with sadness. He was tubercular, and had strong feelings of being doomed to an early death. For this reason also his adaptations of Rubens' sensuousness take on a melancholy and sentimental quality.

The *Italian Comedians* (color plate VIII) is characteristic of Watteau's actual theater pictures. The rich, silky handling of fabric, the solid architectural background, and the well-being and health of the people suggest the Rubens heritage. But the somewhat artificial poses and gestures are from the contemporary theater and its version of the approved manners of the period. The figures are tall, have tiny heads, and are much more self-consciously graceful than in Rubens. Most significant is the air of sadness about the white clown in the center, and the melancholy affection of the young couple at the upper left. This typical mixture of the gay and the sad is characteristic of Watteau as it is of another great Rococo master, the composer Mozart.

Watteau's masterpiece is *The Embarkation for the Isle of Cythera* (fig. 46) for which he was admitted to the French Academy. Here is another, more elaborate presentation of the theme of love. Derived from the theater of that day it is transformed to Watteau's ideal by the magic of flickering chalky drawing, sensitively modeled forms, and delicate features and gestures. On the panoramic canvas the entire stylized code of love-making is summarized. The curious mixture of real and make-believe, so often found in his work, emerges from the rather believable series of episodes in which he has cast his play. Different pairs of young lovers represent the various stages in the process of courtship.

On the extreme right a young man whispers in the ear of an attractive young woman. (They are placed near the symbolic figure of Venus decorated with floral offerings.) Immediately adjacent, another young man raises a young lady to her feet. At the top of the little hillock a third couple is about to descend to join others who are preparing to embark for the Island of Love, but the young lady takes one last lingering look backward. At the lower left the graceful, charming men and women appear against a typical feathery landscape into which their elegant poses and affected manner of love-making blend appropriately. This, suffused with its air of almost intangible sadness, is the spirit of the Rococo on its highest, most sensitive level.

JEAN-BAPTISTE CHARDIN

EARLY in the century, Watteau expressed the ideals of upper class society and laid the groundwork for the Rococo style. Chardin, who was twenty when Watteau died, summed up the aims and aspirations of the rising middle class. His work shows the increasing sense of virtue and self-importance that is evident in bourgeois art, literature, and theater. The conflict reflected in the works of these two men reached its great climax at the end of the eighteenth century in the French Revolution.

In bourgeois art, the painter stresses seriousness instead of charm, sober coloring instead of the brightly flickering effects of Watteau or Fragonard, and subjects that reflect virtue rather than gaiety and stylized love. The middle class artist caters to an element that sees itself as the useful side of society, the side that carries on the business while others idle away their time and the nation's substance.

Born in a poor family in Paris, like many of his eighteenth-century colleagues, Chardin started his career as a decorative painter. Later, as an assistant to J. B. Vanloo, he aided in restoring the pictures in the Great Gallery at Fontainebleau. He first attracted attention with a signboard done for the office of a physician. Instead of the usual medical symbols, Chardin painted a street scene in which a man wounded in a duel is treated by the surgeon—an upper class event depicted in a commonplace way—with people looking on and the physican's office in the background.

His subequent works include simple but intimate do-

47 CHARDIN *Portrait of the Painter*

mestic scenes, still-life pictures with fruits and vegetables, pots, pans, and bottles, as well as some of the most searching psychological portrait studies of the period. This unassuming, self-taught painter emerged from the ordinary life of his time and became its greatest artistic exponent. The influence of Dutch genre painters is apparent in his work, and so, also, is the French tradition of Louis Le Nain.

A series of pictures such as *The Grace Before Meat* shows the more sentimental side of middle class life. However, Chardin made his greatest contribution in paintings like *The House of Cards* (color plate IX). Here are the unaffected honesty, simplicity, and sympathy for the subject that made his art such a novelty and brought him the patronage of middle class customers. The relationship to the Dutch tradition of Vermeer can be seen readily, but the delicacy of drawing, the graceful design, and the large size of the form are quite different. Particularly impressive is the "candid" quality of such scenes; the characters appear unposed and unaware that they are being painted. In Vermeer, one is always conscious of the careful arrangement of form and color, while here one seems to have the opportunity of looking through a window to watch people doing their simple tasks and playing their simple games.

Chardin infused his own kind of atmosphere into these pictures: limpid and clear, like the early paintings of Caravaggio. The simple but effective design enabled him to concentrate on the emotional meaning of the scene. Here a boy is building a house of cards, elsewhere he might be spinning a top. Chardin does not seek to give importance or elegance to the activity, as the Dutch so often do. His purpose is rather to create a mood, gentle and yet strong, of absorption and concentration on the task in hand. His people are enveloped by the poetry of suspended animation which must not be interrupted lest the spell be broken.

In Chardin's compositions, inanimate objects frequently have an importance equal to that of living creatures. The same uniform all-over light bathes people and things and gives his pictures their special textural quality. He does not, however, stress the "touchability" of objects. Rather, he relates them in form and outline to the pattern of the work thereby achieving a more closely knit arrangement. Here, for example, the concentrated light brings the objects together, while the lines flow out along the back and arms of the boy to the cards and return along the scattered objects and through the lines of the table itself.

His portraits also illustrate a simplicity and tranquility different from the general tendencies of the time. The self-portrait (fig. 47), done toward the end of his long life, is a personal and unflattering conception. It shows the artist, a cloth wrapped about his head to protect him from paint, wearing glasses and an eye shade to shield his old eyes. There is no question here of the graces of Watteau or Fragonard with their charming sparkling costumes. Compared with Rococo portraits, Chardin's have an astonishing naturalness and dignity. This is the honest bourgeois who has no use for tinsel, for artificial effects, but must show himself and his time in the most unassuming and straightforward way possible. The informality of the pastel technique, increasingly popular in the eighteenth century also marks a shift from the grand manner of the previous era.

In reply to a painter who tried to tell him how to achieve better colors, Chardin said: "And who told you, sir, that one paints with colors? One makes use of colors, but one paints with the emotions." His great honesty of feeling, so unusual in his own day, became extremely influential later in the century.

JEAN HONORÉ FRAGONARD

Fragonard is the last great painter of the Rococo tradition in France. He is necessarily related to Watteau and Boucher, the earlier artists in this style. But his maturity came in the latter part of the century so that the effects of newer currents are also found in his work.

By the middle of the eighteenth century, middle class feeling in literature and art was quite strong. The sentimental attitude, especially, grew more intense with the approach of the French Revolution which marked the overthrow of the nobility. If Watteau represents the aristocracy at play and Chardin the serious and sober middle class, Fragonard is a sensitive combination of the two points of view. In him the gallant manner of the early part of the century continues on a more serious and sentimental level, as France turns toward the expression of honest feelings and natural attitudes.

Fragonard, born in the town of Grasse, was brought to Paris by his family in 1746. After a brief session as apprentice to a notary, he was sent to the painter Boucher who turned him over to Chardin. Less than pleased with the frivolous character of his pupil, Chardin condemned him as an incorrigible idler who knew only how to spend his time wandering about Paris. The characterization seems to have been apt, and yet, in 1752 Fragonard won the *Prix de Rome*, a much coveted award which enabled him to live and study in Italy. While there he made copies of the

48

FRAGONARD
Bathers

Louvre, Paris

Baroque and Rococo masters, especially Tiepolo from whom he may well have learned the flickering, flowing technique that was to make him outstanding. Later he traveled to Holland where he studied the work of Rembrandt whose brown tonalities and effective light-and-dark treatment left their mark on some of his work.

When Fragonard returned to Paris to begin his professional career, he first attracted attention with a series of openly erotic subjects for which there was a good market. Many, like *The Swing* of the Wallace Collection in London, are a clear indication of what his "not overly scrupulous" brush could produce. Others, like the *Bathers* (fig. 48) of the Louvre, show an equally clear appeal to the senses, though on a more subtle aesthetic level.

The *Bathers* is essentially the same kind of subject as was done by his Rococo predecessors. They, however, relied upon precise draughtsmanship and clear-cut modeling, while Fragonard allows his forms to dissolve in the moving color that surrounds them. With an apparently careless technique, he brings together flecks of light and dark that build up the shape. The action itself is also part of the continuous storm of color and movement.

In a frenzy of exuberant activity, the forms tumble over one another, each presenting some attractive aspect of the female body, each one different in pose and action. Recalling Rubens and his vigorous nudes, we see that Fragonard, like Watteau, etherealized the Flemish painter's vigor. By the same token, the sheer exuberance and physical charm of Fragonard appealed to nineteenth-century painters like Renoir (see *Young Woman in The Sun*, fig. 72) who was affected both technically and spiritually.

Fragonard's bathers, created by little touches of light and shadow, rather than by lines, reproduce the actual process of nature itself. But this is not the slow modulation of light and dark used by the masters of the Renaissance. Fragonard does not wait for the form to evolve. He gives, instead, a series of rapid hints that encircle and suggest the desired shape and make it appear as though by magic.

49 FRAGONARD *The Love Letter*

Fragonard made a lot of money with his widely sought erotic pictures (at one point something like forty thousand pounds a year). But the less sensuous and more sentimental side of his art had an equally great appeal for other groups —that portion of the aristocracy which had turned to a more genuine feeling, as well as for the middle class itself. His series of decorations for the château of Mme. du Barry, the *Development of Love in the Heart of Young Girls* (now in the Frick Museum in New York), shows a more "honest" and serious tone, and a greater sentimentality.

The Love Letter (fig. 49) exemplifies this change. It reveals the almost homey quality which came into his art when, late in life, he married a young girl and settled down. Instead of racy allegories he now offers the gentle and unassuming picture of his own daughter at home, dressed in everyday clothing.

Although the lighting here may be reminiscent in a general way of Vermeer, the total effect is entirely different. The young woman is still a basically charming and even upper class type to whom the painter has added the new qualities of sentiment and mood—but not extravagantly or theatrically as late eighteenth-century middle class painters so often did. Fragonard remains the poet of shadowy effects. The sweeping curves cut across the picture from the window to the right side of the canvas and then down again to the underside of the table which moves in a fine arc to right and left. The dress and other details are painted with an impressionistic handling of the brush. Without lines in the ordinary sense, this creates the illusion of form and movement. The smoothness of such handling suggests the charm of Tiepolo, but the bent form (if it arose it would project out of the picture space) has a curious electric quality which is pure Fragonard.

GIOVANNI BATTISTA TIEPOLO

By the eighteenth century, Venice had become a political and economic backwater without power or influence. The one-time mistress of the Mediterranean, overseer of all east-west trade, was notable primarily as a place for an interesting and picturesque vacation. But, somehow, the city-state had managed to retain its cultural vitality. It had not been touched by the more frenzied religious aspects of the seventeenth-century Baroque. Now, in a period marked by a heightened desire for pleasure, the display and luxury of the Venetian Renaissance tradition of Titian's day were revived and even intensified. Sheltered in an arm of the Adriatic Sea, the lovely city produced its great playwrights like Goldoni, its adventurers like Casanova, its spectacular painters like Tiepolo.

Although Tiepolo's early work is somewhat dark in tone, his later and most characteristic painting has exuberance of color and a light, graceful charm that make him one of the outstanding artists of the Rococo period. A painting like the *Institution of the Rosary* (fig. 50), a fresco done in a Jesuit church, reverts to the procession-like splendor so favored by Venetians of the High Renaissance. It also recalls spectacular ceilings and wall paintings like those of Guercino a century earlier. (See *Aurora*, fig. 31.) But the average Baroque painting is rather heavy in its sense of solemnity and high-seriousness whereas the buoyant charm

50   TIEPOLO   *Institution of the Rosary*

51

TIEPOLO

*Armida
Abandoned by
Rinaldo*

*Courtesy of
The Art Institute of
Chicago*

of everything this artist touches, whether religious or purely allegorical, gives his works their special Rococo quality.

We look straight up into this brilliantly colored and illusionary ceiling. Earlier Venetian artists had shied away from fresco, fearful of painting on wet plaster because of the damp climate of Venice. The medium, however, almost automatically produces the white background which Tiepolo found so useful. On this base, his blues and pinks and yellows stand out with startling clarity and lightness and achieve their extraordinary decorative effect.

Groups of people are cleverly arranged on the mounting steps, carrying the eye back and forth in zigzag fashion. The figures at the bottom represent the Lucifer and his demons repulsed by the rosary. The action moves up to the left through a group sprawled on the stairs, then to the right, where another group is seen partly in brilliant illumination and partly in shadow. It shifts again through the people who symbolize mankind receiving the gift of the rosary from St. Dominic who stands opposite them at the top of the steps. The movement continues upward and left to the Virgin and, in the final reversal to Her cohorts and angels who rise into space.

Even a black and white reproduction shows how bright and luminous the picture is. Tiepolo conceived this solemn religious moment as a spectacle, in the tradition of earlier Venetian art. Life was not to be intimidated by the solemnity of religion. Here are portrayed the charming upper class citizens themselves to make the scene more convincing. more like the material and lavish spectacles to which the city was so accustomed.

Because our traditional religious presentations are serious, Rococo art may not be thought of as suitable for the expression of religious ideals. But Tiepolo's works prove the contrary. His charming and colorful pictures in the churches and palaces of Venice soon made him known throughout Europe. In 1750 he was called to Würzburg in southern Germany to decorate the archbishop's palace. This helped to spread his version of the Rococo style into Bavaria and

Austria where it was very much at home among the elaborately ornamented churches and palaces.

Similarly, he was invited to do the ceiling paintings of the newly finished Royal Palace in Madrid. This brought the Rococo style to Spain and influenced the early work of Goya. The latter's tapestry, cartoons, and decorative religious works show the impact of pictures like *Armida Abandoned by Rinaldo* (fig. 51). A large oil, it is part of a series in which the painter traces a romance in a manner reminiscent of Fragonard's series for Mme. du Barry. The young warrior, torn between love and duty, finally departs with his companions, leaving a desolate Armida on the shore.

The picture has the quality of an eighteenth-century stage set. Simple rock and architectural forms and a bare indication of landscape form one clear mass. Against the lightly twisting outline of the rock the dramatically posed young woman is seen. Her gesture, the leaning tree in the upper section, and the shape of the rock all point to the main group at the right where a sentimental and still reluctant hero is being urged to come along by burly, yet highly decorative warriors. Their positions and the pointing arm vividly seen against a fleecy white cloud carry the eye to the flock of tiny birds that add to the sense of imminent departure. At the extreme right a boat is brought forward to receive them.

Everything is done in terms of dramatically decorative silhouettes, a technique far different from the dissolved forms and swirling light effects of Fragonard. But the patterned elegance of the work, together with the chalky whites, limpid yellows, blues, and reds, make this picture one of the highest expressions of the Rococo ideal.

I BOTTICELLI *Portrait of a Youth*

BOTTICELLI TO VAN GOGH
A PORTFOLIO
OF MASTERPIECES
IN COLOR

II   JAN VAN EYCK   *The Annunciation*

III   RAPHAEL   *Saint George and the Dragon*

IV   TITIAN   *Venus with a Mirror*

PARVVLE PATRISSA, PATRIA, VIRTVTIS ET HÆRES
ESTO, NIHIL MAIVS MAXIMVS ORBIS HABET.
GNATVM VIX POSSVNT COELVM ET NATVRA DEDISSE,
HVIVS QVEM PATRIS, VICTVS HONORET HONOS.
ÆQVATO TANTVM, TANTI TV FACTA PARENTIS,
VOTA HOMINVM, VIX QVO PROGREDIANTVR, HABENT
VINCITO, VICISTI, QVOT REGES PRISCVS ADORAT
ORBIS, NEC TE QVI VINCERE POSSIT, ERIT.

V HANS HOLBEIN, the younger *Edward VI as a Child*

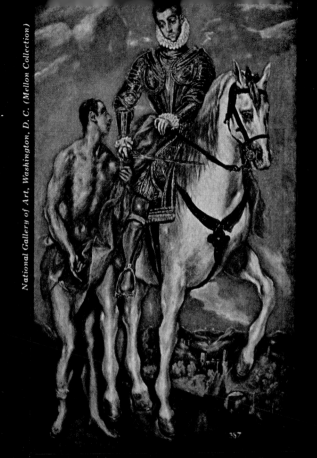

387

VI EL GRECO *Saint Martin and the Beggar*

VII   REMBRANDT   *Self-Portrait*

National Gallery of Art, Washington, D. C. (Mellon Collection)

VIII   WATTEAU   *Italian Comedians*

IX   CHARDIN   *The House of Cards*

X   GAINSBOROUGH   *Mrs. Richard Brinsley Sheridan*

XII CONSTABLE *Wivenhoe Park, Essex*   *National Gallery of Art, Washington, D. C. (Widener Collection)*

XIII   RENOIR   *Oarsmen at Chatou*

XIV

HOMER

Breezing Up

National Gallery of Art, Washington, D. C. (Chester Dale Collection)

XV
CÉZANNE
Still Life

XVI VAN GOGH *La Mousmé*

THOMAS GAINSBOROUGH

Eighteenth-century England produced the sharp criticism of Addison and Steele, the caricatures of Hogarth, and the lusty novels of Smollet, Fielding, and Sterne. But its most popular paintings were society portraits like those of Gainsborough. The apparent paradox was due to the fact that in this fluid and changing society the upper middle classes were the new patrons of art. They wished to be represented by a dignity, grace, and charm which they did not always deserve. English art, still primarily under the influence of older Continental masters, turned to Rubens and his pupil Van Dyck for guidance in the expression of this aristocratic ideal.

Looking at the elegant portraits of Thomas Gainsborough, it is difficult to realize that he himself was far from aristocratic. He was the son of a clothier in Suffolk. At twelve he had been sent to London to study under the painter Hayman, a somewhat questionable character from whom Gainsborough's later inelegant behavior may derive. In the words of one chronicler: ". . . he sometimes used oaths and strayed occasionally from the path of sobriety."

Gainsborough soon set himself up in Hatton Garden as a portrait painter, since this was the only way to make a living as an artist. As a diversion, he painted landscapes. There was still no market for them, but these little pictures are important in the development of English landscape art.

About 1758 he and his wife moved to Bath, a fashionable watering place where he began his career as a society

52

GAINSBOROUGH

Landscape

painter. He spent a number of years there, sending occasional pictures to London. Although by no means well educated, his wit and charm gained him the friendship of many of the literati. When the Royal Academy was established he was among the founding members.

Mrs. Richard Brinsley Sheridan (color plate X) portrays the wife of the brilliant Irish playwright who wrote *The School for Scandal* and *The Critic*. This portrait is a typical example of Gainsborough's mature style. From Van Dyck are derived its elongated proportions and handling of cloth. Though it illustrates the general style of the period, this work has its own individual quality. While Van Dyck conveys the air of a court pageant and most of the English portraitists give a sense of worldly riches and even smugness, Gainsborough imparts a feeling of refinement and delicate breeding. He is not interested in photographic likeness, but rather in the poetic expression of individuality. This attempt to find out what the person really represents, to get beneath the surface, often results in the painter's projecting himself into the character of the sitter just as Leonardo did with the *Mona Lisa*.

There is a consistent suggestion of Watteau in these long graceful figures, with their tiny oval faces and look of inbreeding, and in the subtly delicate manner of handling fabrics. Similarly, Gainsborough's fuzzy landscape backgrounds, here and in many other works, suggest the early Rococo French painter.

If the portrait of Sheridan's wife is transfigured by friendly feeling for the sitter, such is not the case with all of the fashionable portraits he turned out during the years in Bath and London. Gainsborough has described his working method, especially with women. He would ignore the sitter for a long time and instead of trying to get her likeness, would paint the most beautiful creature he could evoke. Then he would work down and away from this idealization until he reached a point where the lovely image on the canvas began to resemble the woman sitting before him— and then he would stop. Although this is probably an exaggeration, one may suppose that many ladies came off better than they deserved. Certainly he was bored by some of these jobs. Gainsborough, who was a sensitive musician, said: "I'm sick of Portraits and wish very much to take my viol-da-gamba and walk off to some sweet village where I can paint landscapes and enjoy the fag end of life in quietness and ease. But these fine ladies and their tea-drinkings, dancings, husband-huntings, etc., etc., etc., will fob me out of the last ten years . . ."

In addition to his love for music and his appreciation of a pretty woman or a good bottle of wine, Gainsborough was devoted to landscape painting. Here he was apparently able to express in an intimate way the delicate and sensitive moods of his extremely volatile temperament. Interest in nature was part of the general eighteenth century turning from the artificial as expressed by Jean Jacques Rousseau and others. With Gainsborough this was no affectation, but a needed emotional outlet.

The *Landscape* (fig. 52) is one of the most poetic and evocative of the entire period. It brings a feeling of unworldliness, of evening quiet, as the little figures move diagonally across the picture, some coming from the small church, others going toward it. A series of broad sweeping curves and generalized hills and a shimmering cool color unite the luminous background of Titian and the great feeling for nature of Rubens. But the color quality and the particular mood are Gainsborough's.

Although this work is a product of the same period as Gray's *Elegy in a Country Churchyard*, the painter's intent is entirely unlike the poet's. Gainsborough shows none of Gray's concern with mortality. Each returns to nature for a different solace; each expresses its beauty and its moods in the language of his own craft.

JOHN SINGLETON COPLEY

THE America of John Singleton Copley was not particularly congenial to the development of the arts. Of Boston he complained: "Were it not for preserving the resemblance of particular persons, painting would not be known in the place." Besides the Puritan restraints placed upon art, the New Englanders considered it "no more than any other useful trade." Yet this man, working without benefit of the instruction available in other countries, without the stimulation of fine collections, became not only the leading portraitist of America but one of the leading painters of his period.

From his stepfather Peter Pelham, who died when the boy was fourteen, Copley learned the basic elements of his craft. He then looked for other sources in the stiff and awkward works of his provincial contemporaries and, more important, in the old masters toward whom he constantly yearned. Available copies of Titian, Van Dyck, Rubens, and Raphael were bad in color but preserved their fine composition. It is also likely that Copley was familiar with engravings after the great portrait painters of the seventeenth century whose rich clothes and dignified gestures are often reproduced in his works. There are also strong reminiscences of early eighteenth-century informality such as that found in the painting of Chardin and Hogarth.

Copley's public was primarily the American upper middle class, which accounts for his unaffected and straightforward psychological approach, his non-Rococo quality. At

53 COPLEY *Portrait of Nathaniel Hurd*

54   COPLEY   *Portrait of Thomas Mifflin and His Wife*

the same time the Boston, New York, and Philadelphia worthies liked to see themselves portrayed with more than mere middle class dignity. Expensive and even sumptuous materials are used for their garments and for the curtained background. The combination of these richly textured materials with a constant informality of pose and expression is one of the unusual features of Copley's art. As the leading portraitist of Boston, he set down the faces of its prominent citizens for some fifteen years. When the first rumblings of the Revolution became audible, he went to England and became a leading figure there also.

The high point of his American period is the final ten years, 1764–74. Here, his remarkable sense of characterization and his feeling for the self-esteem of his middle class sitters emerge in fullest form. As with Chardin, his work is unusual for its tremendous sincerity and directness, its high degree of individualization of each sitter. While the age as a whole produced somewhat stereotyped, formal and fashionable portraiture (see Gainsborough, color plate X), Copley represents quite another point of view. His estimates are warm, intimate, and personalized.

The *Portrait of Nathaniel Hurd* (fig. 53) exemplifies the strong, even monumental sense of form and luxurious quality of fabric that are set off by the informality of pose and the working cap. The practical air of the craftsman contrasts with the books before him. Hurd was the son of a well-known Boston silversmith and he followed his father's profession.

Copley exchanged letters with the Philadelphian Benjamin West, who was already in London, and with the great English painter, Sir Joshua Reynolds. Both these gentlemen wrote in the most extravagant terms, making him even more eager to leave "this frozen region" and bask in the warmth of old masters and London society. But the pictures of those last ten years in America are still the warmest, fullest reflection of the unassuming character of Colonial life and the spirit of the people who were soon to revolt against England. His portrait of his half-brother, known as *The Boy with a Flying Squirrel*, shown in London with great success, has the intimacy and mood of a Chardin.

The magnificent portrait of *Thomas Mifflin and His Wife* (fig. 54) was done in 1773. Mifflin was later a member of the Continental Congress and governor of Pennsylvania; during the Revolution he was Washington's first aide-de-camp and Quartermaster General of the entire army. Here Copley has used the tight drawing and compact organization of Raphael together with his own, unique color gamut of cool metallic tonalities, and his equally personal sense of characterization.

It is said that he painted this picture after seeing a copy of Titian's evocative double portrait, the *Concert*. But where the Venetian painter is romantic, the American artist deliberately shows the everyday activities of the couple, their ease with each other. They are bound together by their poses, the all-over lighting effect, and by the way their arms are arranged in a pattern that moves back and forth.

A good part of Copley's life, from 1774 to 1815, was spent in England, but the great accomplishments belong to his earlier years. Under the influence of formalized English portraiture and fashionable society, his art changed from individual interpretations to what the sitter wished to see. Undeniably he would have remained a greater painter had he stayed in the Colonies.

JACQUES LOUIS DAVID

WITH the increasing aggressiveness of the middle class toward the end of the eighteenth century there arose a new or neo-classical expression based on ancient Roman art. In a relatively short time the two earlier styles, the elegant charming Rococo and the more democratic realism of men like Chardin, had been swept aside in favor of this new approach in painting, sculpture, and architecture.

A number of circumstances contributed to the change. First, important excavations brought to light the ancient cities of Pompeii and Herculaneum, creating a vogue for classical art. Second, bourgeois revulsion against the lightness and frothiness of the aristocratic Rococo style made a more severe and formal approach inevitable. The final factor resulted from a combination of the first two: in the period immediately before the French Revolution artists and writers found in ancient art the reflection of a strongly moral attitude and the echo of a golden age.

Jacques Louis David, the outstanding artist of the French Revolution, used this ancient material to stimulate patriotism among his contemporaries. Even before the Revolution, pictures like *The Oath of the Horatii* (fig. 55) evoked the simplicity and devotion to duty which were popularly associated with republican Rome. Here the painter has arranged his clearly outlined forms across the painting like the semisculptured figures of a bas-relief. Each group is encompassed in its own arch. Simple Roman Doric columns furnish an austere background for the story. In the center is the father, the symbol of middle class family virtue. Dramatically he holds aloft the swords of his sons making them swear they will be faithful to their trust. Patriotism and devotion to country are the keynote. The story is complicated by the fact that these young men are setting out to fight a neighboring city from which come the husbands of their sisters (the weeping ladies at the right). This places duty on a higher plane than devotion to family—a startling idea in the bourgeois eighteenth century, but a sign of the new political virtue. In such themes as Brutus condemning his own sons to death for crimes against the state, David again poses this same problem.

The Oath of the Horatii was presented in 1785, while David was still a court painter to Louis XVI. It was the sensation of that season. This work, with a number of subsequent pictures, are believed to have contributed significantly to rousing revolutionary sentiment. When the Revolution broke out in 1789, David became one of its leading figures. He joined the Jacobin Club and in 1792 was elected to the National Convention, of which he soon became the secretary. As a member of the Committee of Public Safety, he voted for the execution of his former employer, the king, an act that was completely consistent for the painter of Brutus Mourning the Death of His Sons. David organized and designed all revolutionary celebrations and for a brief time was even President of the Convention.

In 1793 when one of the deputies, St. Fargeau, was assassinated, David painted him on his deathbed. The picture was hung in the Convention hall as a portrait of "the first martyr of liberty." Some six months later Charlotte Corday stole into the apartment of Marat, the great friend of the people, and stabbed him to death as he sat in his bath. Once more the Convention called upon David and this time he painted the famous The Death of Marat· (fig. 56), a tribute to a personal friend whom he had visited in his home only the day before.

Here David shows the other side of his talents. This is not a harsh-colored imitation of Roman bas-relief sculp-

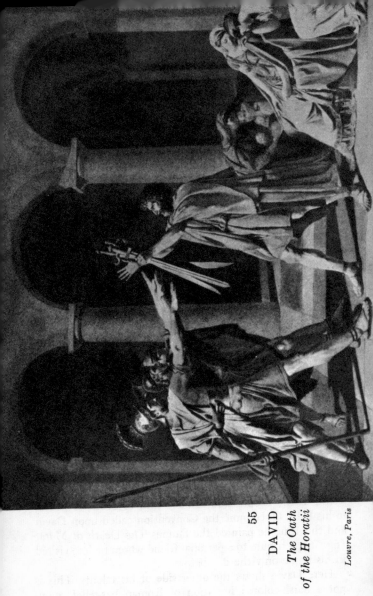

55
DAVID
*The Oath
of the Horatii*

Louvre, Paris

ture, but a dramatically conceived Baroque martyrdom, realistically painted and designed to evoke pity. The great revolutionary is slumped back; the illumination comes from the upper left as in Caravaggio. The top of the face and the left side of the figure are brightly lit, leaving the upper part of the body in shadow. The light moves on to the left arm and to the hand that holds a letter from the lady who stabbed him.

In the interest of greater effectiveness, David emphasizes the actual circumstances of this event: Marat in his bath where he handled much of his correspondence, the towel about his head, the inkwell and quill pens, the knife on the floor, and the meticulous accuracy of the wooden box at the right. As with his previous neo-classical pictures, the exact detail made this work more convincing in the eyes of his public.

In paintings of this kind David follows the naturalistic direction of such eighteenth-century masters as Chardin— a realism that David's own neo-Classical efforts were to kill for quite a long time. Because the ancient and dignified classical style became associated with the triumph of the middle class Revolution, it was rather firmly fixed for the next few generations. Not until the middle of the nineteenth century was French realism revived.

David lived through the entire Revolution, getting in trouble on one occasion but surviving into the period of Napoleon, for whom he also worked. With the end of the Napoleonic era and the return of the Bourbons to France, David went into exile. He died in Belgium.

56 DAVID *The Death of Marat*

FRANCISCO GOYA
Y LUCIENTES

ALTHOUGH he was born before 1750, Goya's art belongs to the nineteenth century. He is one of the first great artists of that period and one of the most influential as well. His methods affected the Romantic tradition of the early nineteenth century, the Realism of the generation after that, the Impressionism of the 1860's, and perhaps even the Expressionism and Surrealism of our own day. Masters like Daumier and Manet freely acknowledge this debt to Goya in their paintings.

The product of a still feudal Spain, Goya portrayed its court life and personages with his own special brand of malice. He also left flaming testimonials to the brutalities of the Napoleonic invasion of his country. Although he grew up in the Velásquez tradition of unadorned naturalism, Goya's work is never objective and scarcely ever is it static. Either biting social commentary or dynamic emotional expressiveness is its purpose; sometimes the two are combined.

Born in the northern province of Aragon, Goya began his studies in Saragossa the nearest large town. When he was not yet twenty he fled to Madrid, under somewhat mysterious circumstances. Legend speaks of a street brawl between two rival parishes in which three boys were killed. There is also some word of difficulties with the Inquisition, but proof for either tale is lacking. When Goya arrived in Madrid in 1766, the Italian painter Tiepolo had already begun the decoration of the Royal Palace. Goya was taken on as one of his assistants. This connection with the crisp, decorative, and brilliantly colored art of the great Venetian had an important effect on the tapestry cartoons of Goya and his early portraits and religious scenes. Goya soon found it desirable to leave Madrid rather hurriedly too. Apparently his wild and dissolute ways were again the cause, for the story is that he was found one morning with a knife between his shoulder blades. He seems to have joined a company of traveling bullfighters and made his way to Italy. The late Baroque art of Rome, with its expressive lighting effects and unusual perspective also influenced the later dramatic work of this painter.

When Goya returned to Madrid, he settled down and married the sister of a well-known neo-classical painter, Bayeu. Although cold sculpturesque forms and Roman subject matter had become extremely popular Goya seems to have favored the more sprightly approach of his former chief, Tiepolo. His first official commission was for a series of cartoons or designs for tapestries that were to be made in the royal factories. In these street and village scenes he recalls the Venetian trick of silhouetting forms and trees against a simple background or high sky. The striking effect produced is altogether suitable for the simple outlines necessary in tapestry.

Goya soon became one of the court painters. His problem—to set down the royal countenance as a thing of dignity—was even worse than that of Velásquez. The latter's patrons had been backward and stupid; those of Goya were all that and were vicious and corrupt besides. Spain was beginning to feel the effects of the stagnant seventeenth century. The great days of colonial and world mastery were long past, and there was an absence of any sort of enterprise, either intellectual or commercial.

The *Portrait of Maria Luisa, Queen of Spain* (fig. 57) utilized the Velásquez technique of a blank background, against which the figure stands out in silhouette. Roundness of form again is restricted to those elements that are

57 GOYA *Portrait of Maria Luisa, Queen of Spain*

not clothed, especially the face and arms. Like the earlier painter, Goya tried to subordinate interpretation to the lavishness of costume: jewels, fan, the aigret which rises from the loose headdress, the rich yellow of the gown, and the jeweled order of the Starred Cross. But it is almost impossible (and this is also true of Velasquez's *Philip IV*) for a naturalistic-minded painter to avoid conveying some element of the sitter's character, no matter how objective he tries to be. Thus the gross and unappetizing quality of the "Spanish Catherine the Great" comes through in this official estimate.

Incapable of flattering his royal patrons Goya attempted to present them in purely visual terms. He presented form emerging in the contrast between light and dark, as Velasquez had done—and as Manet would do in the century following. His portraits of friends and patrons, however, have a more interpretive and sympathetic quality, as in the *Marquesa de Pontejos* (color plate XI) with its reminiscences of Gainsborough and Tiepolo.

Utterly different is the imaginative and critical side of Goya's art. In scenes of wild and grotesque fantasy—the pictures of witches, inquisitions and monsters—he rises to tremendously expressive heights that bring him into the forefront of the Romantic movement. Most exciting perhaps is the long series of fanciful yet socially critical etchings and aquatints, the *Caprices*. Though contemporary events are only hinted at in an indirect way, the cleverly pointed satire is scarcely concealed. Their vivid transitions between dark and light are found again in later aquatints like the *Disasters of War*. These, however, depict the life of the time in a direct and unequivocal fashion.

Goya also did a number of paintings based on the same military events pictured in the *Disasters*. These portray the Napoleonic invasion of Spain in all its horror. The *Execution of the Citizens of Madrid* (fig. 58) is a night scene showing the mass murders committed by the soldiers of General Murat. The firing squad is arranged in a straight line, seen mostly from the back. We are directly confronted

58

GOYA
*Execution of
the Citizens
of Madrid*

Prado, Madrid

by the pathetic, and horror-stricken, victims. Some have already been shot, others cannot look at what is happening, still others face their executioners, urging them to shoot and end the horror. The hill behind these doomed men sweeps down sharply to the right. Its curve is interrupted by an equally powerful thrust in the opposite direction, the line made by the heads of the anonymous executioners. This ends in the white silhouette of the brave Spaniard facing them, who dies for the privilege of fighting back.

JOHN CONSTABLE

Wɪᴛʜ John Constable, the first great landscape painter of nineteenth-century Europe, there emerged a distinct British art. His work and that of his colleagues unmistakably express the English fondness for the outdoors,—their ability to see nature clearly, yet with warmth and tenderness. This highly individual approach exerted a profound influence on several Continental schools.

Gainsborough's eighteenth-century landscapes had expressed a definite point of view about the relationship between the individual and nature; his tiny figures are lost against the vastness of the scene. As the writings of Rousseau and others testify, the English were not alone in this feeling for the immensity of nature. But they were the first to pictorialize their feelings—not only in the fuzzy Watteau-like effects of Gainsborough, but in an increasingly fresh and spontaneous way.

Part of the change came about through the popularity of water-color painting in the latter part of the eighteenth century. Young women and men went out in droves to set down their reactions to nature through a medium that in itself showed the benefits of bright clear painting. This was a considerable step away from the brownish landscapes of Dutch seventeenth-century painters which had been widespread and influential. In 1802 John Crome founded the first art colony for landscape painting. But the full naturalistic potential of the art remained to be worked out by Constable.

59 CONSTABLE *The Hay Wain*

Born in Suffolk, the son of a well-to-do miller, he completed elementary school and went to work in his father's mill. His desire to draw brought him to the attention of the local gentry, one of whom showed the young man's work to Thomas Girtin, leader of the amateur water-color movement.

In 1795 at the age of nineteen Constable went to London, spent two years studying without apparent results, and returned to the mill. He continued to sketch in his spare time. When he was twenty-three, these studies enabled him to enter one of the Royal Academy schools. Within a few years his pictures were being accepted for the Academy shows. Personal and financial difficulties continued, however, and it was not until 1816 that Constable married and settled down to a profitable existence. His art and fame developed to the fullest and he contributed substantially to the popularity of a newer and more spontaneous art form.

Wivenhoe Park, Essex, (color plate XII), an early work, suggests Dutch landscapes in its yellowish foliage and the precise details. Yet a consciousness of the reflections in objects adjacent to each other already gives a greater reality to this picture. The houses and trees on the bank of the river are mirrored in the water, as are the people in the tiny boat.

Compared with the classical French landscapes of Poussin, Constable conveys a sense of intimacy and warmth. He brings us into the picture through the fence and through the foreground shadows that draw us forward. The trees at left move across the picture, carry us along with them. In contrast, French landscape was a symbol rather than a portrayal of nature, the background for poetic evocations of a far distant and unattainable past.

Constable's feeling for the immediacy and movement of air, clouds, and water is developed further in *The Hay Wain* (fig. 59). This was exhibited with a number of other English landscapes in the Paris salon of 1824 where, to a nature-starved public, they were sensational.

In addition to setting the picture in motion, Constable's

color here shows a new freshness. The greens especially are now used in a variety of tones for contrast and interest. Reflections of the trees, houses, and sky, as well as the wagon and boat, add to the feeling of movement in this sparkling work. Instinctively perhaps, Constable placed certain spots of color side by side to reinforce each other—red, and green, for instance.

Pictures of this kind had their effect on the Continent in the French Barbizon school of the 1830–50 period. But another type of picture represents Constable's most spontaneous effort; his "sketches" were influential in the outdoor Impressionism of the 1870's in France. These are rapidly made records of a visual experience in which it is possible to see the path of the artist's brush and to separate the individual spots of color.

The *Salisbury Cathedral* (fig. 60) is a good example of Constable's ability to put together in a relatively hasty manner his visual impression of a particular scene. Here he is really able to show the flickering and momentary character of a landscape, the constant motion of nature as light breezes ruffle the water and move the leaves. Clouds seem to be crossing the sky, instead of acting merely as parts of a composition. Constable's delight in nature appears in a more vivid and exciting way than ever before, either in his own art or that of any other painter.

In some cases, including *Salisbury Cathedral*, he went on to "finish" the picture—to work in a mass of tiny details such as are found in *The Hay Wain*—but this adds nothing to the final result. The wonder of Constable's contribution lies rather in the so-called sketches into which we are projected with stunning effect. In these, we feel ourselves surrounded by a nature in constant and eternal movement.

JOSEPH MALLORD WILLIAM TURNER

J. M. W. TURNER is the fullest, richest, most flamboyant figure in the history of English art. Prodigal in his work as in his life, he nevertheless accumulated more money than any other artist in history and left one of the largest personal collections of paintings, prints, and drawings the world has ever seen. The fabulous energy and drive of this man produced a fortune of about a half-million pounds (in present day values), two hundred finished paintings, about twenty thousand sketches, and innumerable etchings.

The son of a London barber in Maiden Lane, Turner spent most of his life overcoming his background. He consciously set himself up as a rival of the old masters, equalling them in some cases, exceeding them in others. Although he painted many different types of pictures, his great contribution lies in the atmospheric landscape typical of the English and in an altogether personal landscape that differentiates him from all other painters.

The family barber shop was near an art academy and at the age of five Turner was already drawing. Later he wandered about the docks, stealing aboard ships and storing up impressions. By his early teens he was professionally coloring other artists' engravings and architectural sketches. At eighteen he had his own studio and soon afterward went on a walking tour with Thomas Girtin, making drawings along the way and selling them. He had already been exhibiting at the Royal Academy for three years.

From about 1800, Turner began to imitate and challenge the masters of the seventeenth century: the Dutch sea painters and the French and other classical landscapists with their picturesque ruins. In 1802 at the age of twenty-seven he was made a member of the Royal Academy. Now he took his first Continental tour, sailing up and down the coasts of Europe in coal and fishing boats. Turner's purpose in these tours was not to visit art galleries and ancient buildings but rather to store up impressions. Once, the story goes, he had himself lashed to the mast during a storm for four hours so he could see what was happening. Throughout, the main element of his interest was atmospheric light. This element may be used purely to describe a scene; it may give either a gentle or powerful emotive reaction; or it may serve a symbolic and essentially modern purpose.

On the more descriptive side, the *Venice: Dogana and San Giorgio Maggiore* (fig. 61) follows Constable in the portrayal of sunlight and the exploitation of reflections and movements. It also shows the increasing tendency toward color brightness that began with Constable. But the latter relied on various spotting techniques, whereas Turner's method is quite different. Here, for example, the paint is handled in a continuous soft surface manner, leading from one area to another without revealing just how the artist accomplished this. A visual impression and physical feeling of a sun-drenched scene has been achieved. The light is so powerful that it literally swamps every element in the picture. Thus the Dogana (customs house) and the church of San Giorgio at the right are so brightly colored that they tend to disappear in the intense light—as actually happens in real life. Similarly the various objects on the canal have reduced clarity for the same reason. The canal itself is no longer water but a series of reflections from these objects and from the sweeping sky that seems to continue down into the water. Nature and man are combined by the all-consuming power of the sun into a forceful, vividly glowing whole.

To the Impressionists of the later nineteenth century—

61

TURNER

*Venice:
Dogana and
San Giorgio
Maggiore*

*National Gallery of
Art, Washington, D. C.
(Widener Collection)*

62

TURNER

*Rain, Steam
and Speed*

Monet, Pissarro, and Renoir—the work of Turner is important for its atmospheric quality. Together with Constable they hailed him as a predecessor and patron saint. But unlike them, Turner is a product of the Romantic era; he is just as concerned with the power and majesty of natural forces as with their atmospheric possibilities.

Thus, here and in later works such as the *Whale Ship*, the *Snow Storm*, or the *Rain, Steam and Speed* (fig. 62), he produces something altogether unique artistically, but entirely in keeping with the period. In these paintings he has devised a means of representing forces that have no actual form, such as the storm, the violence of the sea, rain, or steam and speed. This is a far more dynamic conception than anything in the entire range of English landscape painting, which had progressed from the idylls of Gainsborough through the atmospheric pictures of Constable to this new abstract and violent conception of nature.

The *Rain, Steam and Speed* shows a train rushing across a bridge, the thick fog swirling about it, the red glow of its furnace standing out against the enveloping mist. In such portrayals form is of little importance in the attempt to get at the inner meaning of an idea. Here, or in the *Whale Ship*—which expresses the essence of struggle with its bloodied waters—Turner is closer to twentieth-century Expressionists like Kokoschka (fig. 90) than to the atmospheric-minded Impressionists of the nineteenth century.

EUGÈNE DELACROIX

ROMANTICISM was the impassioned revolt against all that would restrict man's development. It stood for the expression of individual personality on a high emotional plane, whether in art, literature, or music. In painting, it might be the artist's own personality (and his right of self-expression), the personality of an oppressed Greek fighting against the Turks, or the personality of some literary figure that appealed to the painter because of its "problem" aspect.

Toward that end the French painters of the period devised a technique like the Baroque. Their bright colors, sharp diagonal movements, constantly moving forms, and melodramatic lighting suggest the combined effects of Rubens, Caravaggio, and other seventeenth-century masters. Rembrandt used his mysterious illumination to express a personal philosophy and Caravaggio his dramatic lighting to express pathos; Rubens employed a richly sensuous and brilliantly colored art to express a more dynamic and emotional quality. French Romantic painters gravitated toward those styles for somewhat similar purposes.

The most important of these painters was Eugène Delacroix, a highly cultured and sensitive individual. His emotive, forceful, and colorful formulation was rejected by critics of his time who said that he painted "with a drunken broom." Today the style of Delacroix appears by no means violent and we can more soberly appreciate his sympathy for the poor and oppressed.

Though the Napoleonic era had been followed by a period of disillusion and political reaction, people like Delacroix still felt that a better world could be built. In spite of the attempts of conservatives to wipe out the gains of the Revolution during the first half of the nineteenth century, many liberal writers and artists continued to speak for individual freedom.

For the artist there was greater opportunity to exhibit his pictures, but the tastes he had to cater to were those of a rather uninformed middle class. This group, once the vanguard of revolt, had now become an element of conservatism. In art their preferences rested stolidly on the older classical masters. Every attempt to do something different, to express the dynamic new quality of the nineteenth century, was violently opposed. Like the writing of Byron, Hugo and Shelley, the new individualistic painting was soon associated in the public mind with political radicalism. Actually Byron, Delacroix and many of their contemporaries were definitely on the side of the underdog and sprang immediately to the defense of the oppressed.

Delacroix's *The Massacre at Scio* (fig. 63) was shown at the official 1824 salon where Constable and his friends exhibited their bright clean landscapes. It was received by some critics as the "massacre of painting." This reaction is entirely understandable from men whose standards were based on the neo-classical severity of David's cold color and carefully drawn sculpturesque forms. For Delacroix, on the other hand, the problem was to express his deep compassion for the oppressed Greeks and to show as vividly as possible their sufferings.

On one side is a rising pyramid of the sick and the weary. From this heap of tortured human beings the form of a man leads us to the right. Here another pyramid rises sharply; at its top a Turkish horseman carries off a beautiful girl. In the background, smoke covers the still smoldering ruins of a city. At the bottom of the right-hand group, the painter shows a dead mother and a child crawling over her. For conservative people the unusual brilliance

63   DELACROIX   *The Massacre at Scio*

of Delacroix's painting, its vivid touches of color placed side by side, was just as much of a shock as the brutality and realism of the scene itself. To Delacroix and his fellow-Romantics, here was a group of suffering people that had to be helped. Delacroix did it with his painting, Byron with his poetry and then by joining the Greeks in their war for independence.

The struggle between conservatives and liberals reached a climax in the Revolution of 1830. A year later Delacroix presented his famous *Liberty Leading the People* (fig. 64). A striking mixture of allegory and realism, it shows the powerful and beautiful semi-nude figure of Liberty moving across the barricades. At her side a boy brandishes a pair of pistols and shouts his defiance. On the left are a laborer with a sword and an office worker (wearing the high hat of that day) with a rifle; they move forward in the vanguard of the advancing revolutionaries.

The element of pathos appears in the dead and dying figures around the barricade and the wounded man who crawls upward toward the shining figure of Liberty. But this is a far more powerful and assertive statement than *The Massacre at Scio*. Here the painter glorifies the idea of revolt. At the same time the element of horror is more striking than in the earlier picture, and is reminiscent of Goya's *Execution of the Citizens of Madrid* (fig. 58).

With the conservative triumph after the 1830 Revolution, it became inadvisable for painters to express themselves so directly. The Romantics as a group took refuge in escapism, showing dissatisfaction with the times by running away from them. Delacroix now drew subjects from literary sources that offered him the consolation of times long past as well as the noncontroversial individual problems of fictional heroes. This phase of his activity is exemplified in *Hamlet and Horatio*, featuring the indecision of the melancholy Dane, or the *Abduction of Rebecca*, showing the anguish, tumult, and excitement of that scene from Scott's *Ivanhoe*.

In addition to literary pictures, Delacroix and others also

64

DELACROIX
*Liberty Leading
the People*

Louvre, Paris

used picturesque scenes from the Near East. These ventures into the distance were another means of escape from the uncongenial and unhappy environment surrounding intellectuals of that time.

GUSTAVE COURBET

By the middle of the nineteenth century material and industrial progress was being directly reflected in the works of writers and painters. Mechanization brought an ever growing interest in the physical nature of things and in the problem of man against the world. The great developments in science were now paralleled by a concern with the new social and philosophical problems. In art there appeared a mass of works which, though still concerned with the fate of individual man, were increasingly aware of physical environment. There is less tendency to idealize in the manner of the neo-classicists or glamorize and dramatize like the Romantics. By the 1850's neither sculpturesque figures of ancient times nor pictureque Algerians or Shakespearean characters were adequate for the needs of this new period.

Courbet was one of the most outspoken defenders of the Realistic attitude in painting. The son of a well-to-do provincial family, he came to Paris in 1839 to study art. His early work in the big city, most of it without formal teaching, was Romantic. *Monk in a Cloister, Ruins by a Lake*, and *Despair* indicate that he was a man of the time.

Realistic painting in France began to come into its own after the 1848 Revolution. Courbet's contribution was in two works rather unusual for that time: *The Stone Breakers* and *After Dinner at Ornans*. The first is an ordinary scene of two country folk breaking stones for road mending. The dark-colored and deliberately commonplace treatment annoyed both Classicists and Romantics but it remained

65 COURBET *Man with the Leather Belt*

66 COURBET *Young Bather*

the basis of his approach. The *After Dinner at Ornans* has an atmospheric mood and a feeling of suspended animation that go back to Louis Le Nain in the seventeenth century (fig. 41). This interest in mood is the other side of Courbet's personality as an artist.

In his vehement insistence on the right of the individual to say and do what he liked, Courbet remained basically a Romantic. His refusal to paint anything he could not see is an equally dogmatic assertion of his own importance. (It recalls Caravaggio tying wings on his angel models.) His great egotism is further shown in his love for painting himself. Everywhere possible he inserts his own face and figure, not merely as an incidental character but as the center of attention. His formal self-portraits, such as the one in the Louvre (fig. 65), are among the century's most persuasive expositions of the importance of the individual.

In this regard Courbet's self-estimates are considerably different from those of artists like Titian and Rembrandt (color plate VII). These men were concerned with the presentation of a dignified individual or with a philosophical viewpoint. Courbet, on the other hand, is interested in the projection of his own personality in the typical Romantic fashion of Byron, Chopin, and Delacroix. But he is far more self-conscious and aggressive in the social and materialistic sense than any of the others. Wherever Courbet shows his own face, it is with a self-assertive independence. Here this emerges from the tilt of the head, the angle of the hands and the violent twist of the shoulders. Technically it is still dependent on the seventeenth century: Caravaggio, Frans Hals, and other great realists of that epoch.

In Courbet's time it was considered "advanced" to assert that the artist had the right to paint anything he wanted, no matter how ordinary. Pictures like *The Stone Breakers* or the famous *Burial at Ornans*, with its everyday and unsacred presentation of various types of people at a small-town funeral, earned for Courbet the title "Realist." In the Paris of the 1850's and 1860's this was as damning as being called a Socialist.

To a classically inclined public, pictures like the *Young Bather* (fig. 66) were very annoying. Today its mixture of the pastoral and the sensual has a pleasant, if not overwhelming quality. For the spectators of 1866, it was an affront to their sense of propriety. Instead of the conventional slick, slim, and beautifully proportioned neo-classical nude that has nothing to do with reality, Courbet tried to portray what he saw. He presented a plump, realistically bulging young creature. Not conventional linear continuity and ideal proportion but rather the sheer physical appeal of the form, and its touch qualities is accentuated. The shape of individual parts and the surface handling of the skin with its slightly oily quality convey a visual response.

One might say that Courbet treated the nude not only in an unglamorous fashion (contrast Titian, fig. 20), but almost as a piece of still life. Yet, since he is an emotional human being, even this young woman emerges with a somewhat sentimental and pastoral air. As she leans forward to put her toe in the water, the left arm extends along the branch and gives the body an attractive curve following the shape of the landscape background.

Courbet's contribution lay in turning people's minds toward the material at a time when they were still hemmed in by either Classical artificiality or Romantic exaggeration. His aggressive attitude and leadership made it clear that the independent artist was an important social entity with a right to free expression.

HONORÉ DAUMIER

A CONTEMPORARY and fellow-Realist of Courbet, Honoré Daumier was an altogether different sort of man. In contrast to the former's middle class background, egotism, and political posturing, Daumier was a poor man, self-effacing, and politically serious. Whereas Courbet appointed himself leader of the forces of progress, Daumier remained almost completely unknown to the public. Nor was he an exponent of Realism for its own sake, for the touch qualities of substances. Daumier's Realism is on a higher, more expressive level. He is a far deeper thinker than Courbet, more aware of the reasons for social injustice and quite ready to portray them. His painting is both Realistic and philosophic.

The son of a poor glazier, Daumier had to help support his family. As a child, he was apprenticed to a process server. This experience showed him the corruption of the courts and also the great variety of Parisian life. While still a boy, he learned the technique of lithography, through which drawings on stone can be reproduced, and earned extra money in commercial art work.

His career began with the satirical cartoons which he drew for one of the opposition newspapers. After the failure of the Revolution of 1830, he went to jail for six months for doing a caricature of the king. When in the course of the 1834 civil disturbances, the police shot a number of innocent people in an apartment house, Daumier did a powerful cartoon of this event. The famous *Rue Trans-*

nonain was a clear indictment of official brutality. After the Revolution of 1848 he continued his attacks on corruption and injustice under Louis Napoleon.

For more than forty years Daumier produced his pictorial comments, attacking opportunists and thieves of all kinds. To these creatures he gave harsh treatment, but his attitude toward the "little man" was a mixture of irony and pity. His work as a painter is related in feeling and form to his lithography although it is not nearly as topical in impact. The paintings lacked the pressure of the weekly deadline and thus could be broader and more philosophical in approach. Even though he was tied to a job for most of his life the variety and quantity of these works is impressive.

Daumier's sympathy for the poor is expressed in the *Third Class Carriage* (fig. 67). A group of ordinary people sit in a train going between the suburbs and the big city. Whereas Turner made his train a symbol of power, Daumier is interested in people and their relationships. Facing us are two peasant women, the younger holding a sleeping child. The old woman has a straw basket around which her hands lie in a simple resting position. Near her a tired little boy slumps sideways in sleep. Light comes from the window at the left, falling primarily on these two monumentalized women.

There is no question here of photographic detail. The broad general treatment stresses the largeness and heroic quality of these plain folk, the quiet pleasure of the young mother, and the impassive dignity of the older woman. Behind them are other characters of the big city. The men in high hats represent office workers, while simpler types are shown in skull caps and bowlers. They meet for a moment in the train, intent on where they are going, soon to be dispersed.

Daumier has given these people the dignity with which Le Nain invested his peasants centuries earlier (fig. 40). But this is a new social group and a new technique. The transition from a very light to a very dark area without

67

DAUMIER

*Third Class
Carriage*

Courtesy of
The Metropolitan
Museum of Art,
New York

the usual gradual modulation is a feature of Daumier's method. It may derive from his habit of modeling figures in clay and is also affected by Goya.

In addition to scenes of this type, Daumier has done many mood-filled paintings of clowns, lawyers, art lovers, and bathers—all with the same largely conceived and executed figures, all with an emotion to convey. These may be considered genre or everyday subjects, whatever their expressive intent. There are also the philosophical or literary pictures in which he portrays such abstract ideas as greed, violence, or idealism.

The many versions of *Don Quixote* (fig. 68) are not drawn from a commonplace situation which is then elevated to a broader significance. Here the universal truth of a literary subject is directly pictorialized. In this example the individuals are more abstract than in the *Third Class Carriage*. The bulk of the form is reduced to a vibrant twist of outline. The figure of the idealistic Don Quixote is a bold dark area against the luminous sky, as he goes forward with lance raised. The fat squire Sancho Panza coming over the hill is a disconsolate blot of color on his donkey. Landscape also is simplified. The large areas are set off from each other in a clear and nonphotographic manner. As the knight on his white Rosinante moves down into the picture toward the dead horse in the road, the background hills carry the eye back into the picture space. A balance is established, like that between the temperaments of Don Quixote and Sancho Panza, symbols of the diversity of human aspiration.

68 DAUMIER *Don Quixote*

ÉDOUARD MANET

The art of Édouard Manet marks a real break with the past; in many ways he is the first modern painter. In his own times he was considered another Realist and shared with Courbet the notoriety of that movement. During the 1860's he became the leader of a new group of dissident artists, the so-called Impressionists.

Courbet's primary concern was with subject matter; technically, his art went back to the seventeenth century. Manet, on the other hand, was much more concerned with technical effects, particularly natural light. What he painted was relatively unimportant, so long as it made an interesting arrangement of form and color. His subject was not a matter for social or moral uplift but rather what artists call a *motif* or arrangement. The logical conclusion of this attitude, which may be seen during our own time, is to ignore the subject completely, in favor of method and form.

The Realist was excited about his right to paint *whatever* he liked. The newer Impressionists, led at first by Manet, were interested in their right to paint *however* they liked. There was some scandal about two of Manet's pictures which were attacked on the ground of immorality (as well as method). But the bulk of Impressionist painting is a colorful and charming expression of the life of the big city and the suburbs around it. The paintings of Manet, Monet, Degas, Renoir, and others offer a new series of subjects derived from city life and handled in a vibrant and momentary fashion. They express the nature of metro-

69

MANET

*Luncheon
on the Grass*

Louvre, Paris

politan living in a quite different way from the solid bulky forms of Daumier and Courbet.

The Impressionist group was organized shortly after the Revolution of 1870. Since most people did not understand what they were trying to do, they were labeled subversive. The fact that Manet, Renoir, and others were nonpolitical, that Degas was a last-ditch conservative, and Cézanne a good Catholic, did not deter their attackers.

The "realism" of Manet shows the figure as it appears in natural light and in contrast to its background. His primary interest is the initial visual impression—what one sees in the first moment of looking at anything, when the eye has not yet had time to absorb the figure and give it roundness. Manet was first brought to public attention by the famous *Luncheon on the Grass* (fig. 69). Today this painting is enshrined in the Louvre but in 1863 it was the subject of violent attack. It was rejected for the official salon of that year, together with a number of other works, and by the order of Louis Napoleon was put into the "Salon of the Refused."

Since it brought together in one space a nude young woman with two clothed young men and a half dressed girl in the background it could be attacked on the ground of immorality. Conservative critics found it easy to incite the public against such a picture. It was, they admitted, very much like the *Pastoral Concert* of Giorgione in the Louvre but "not idealized." This in itself made it a criminal offense. To add insult to injury, there was an undecorative mess of half-eaten food at the lower left-hand corner of the picture. The traditionalists were further enraged because Manet, in his search for a natural light effect, had developed an altogether new technique.

The artists of the past had worked from a dark underpainting to a series of highlights. They added glaze after glaze in order to achieve the illusion of form. Manet felt that the results of this system could never be natural and bright enough. He therefore turned the method upside down and began with a bright underpainting as his first

coat. He added a series of half-darks and darks as he went along, while the brightly colored background was still wet. This often gave the result of charging his canvas with light since the underpainting would reflect light back into the eye of the spectator.

Besides this revolutionary approach, the people in the picture are shown almost without shadow. They are flat silhouetted forms momentarily visualized as the eye of the spectator catches them. This also agitated the entrenched salon artists, as was indicated by the reception accorded Manet's celebrated *Olympia* two years later. Here a flatly modeled, brilliantly lighted nude looks straight at the audience, while her maid brings the daily bunch of flowers from her protector. Actual physical attacks were made on the picture and Manet had to leave the country for a while.

When he returned, Émile Zola, then a budding young journalist, singled out his *The Fifer* (fig. 70) for special praise. It was a courageous thing to do even though this painting reveals the heritage from Velásquez and Goya. This is apparent in the flatness of visualization and the contrast between the figure and the background against which it is silhouetted. As in the works of the Spaniards, only the face and the hands are given the benefit of modeling. The rest of the body is left relatively flat—as indeed it would look at the first moment.

The picture is also remarkable for its elegant decorative form. It suggests the suavity and charm of Persian miniatures, both in the brilliant color effects and in the way the figure has been reduced to an abstract pattern swinging right and left. Emotional content is relatively unimportant. This "art for art's sake" attitude anticipates many twentieth-century masters to whom the motif and its handling are the significant element—not the subject or its feelings.

PIERRE AUGUSTE RENOIR

Outdoor Impressionism, the art of enveloping a subject in an atmosphere of shimmering and clean color, was the joint creation of Pierre Auguste Renoir and Claude Monet. During the early 1870's these two artists developed a method of bringing together little spots of unmixed color that would reinforce each other. This produced a highly light-charged, flickering, and momentary "impression" of the object viewed. In its concern with the function of natural light, this art parallels the painting of Edouard Manet. In actual method, however, it substitutes tiny spots of pure color (as it comes from the tube) for the broad flat color areas of the older painter.

Renoir and Monet, as well as Pissarro and Sisley, represent a joyous, even lyrical approach to reality that belies the actual appearance of late nineteenth-century Paris. The city and its suburbs are given a pleasurable, colorful, and richly vibrating quality. Yet, since their technique was a deviation from the accepted form, their pictures were scorned by the critics and public of that day. Their art, which is the most pleasant pictorial interpretation of modern life, remained outside the conventional art world for almost a generation. Following on the heels of the Manet scandals, the new Impressionist pictures were also the victims of organized hostility. Intolerant criticisms, music hall skits, newspaper ridicule, and political defamation took their usual course.

Renoir's fully developed style is broader in scope than

72 RENOIR *Young Woman in the Sun*

the outdoor Impressionist method he evolved with Monet. His art is steeped in the tradition of the great masters— Titian, Rubens, Fragonard—indeed of all who have celebrated the joy of living in general and the beauty of women in particular. He represents a fusion of old and new techniques. Unlike the usual outdoor Impressionist paintings whose figures often tend to be lost in a haze of shimmering atmospheric color, his works are substantial in form and design.

Renoir was the son of a poor tailor who had brought his family from Limoges to Paris when the boy was four. At the age of thirteen he was apprenticed to a porcelain painter from whom he may have acquired his taste for the brilliant blues he used in his later work. In the shop he copied pretty flowers and figures, while in his spare time he did sketches from classical sculptures at the Louvre. He was ready to become a professional porcelain painter at seventeen, but a mechanical method for doing the work was invented and he was out of a job. He turned to the painting of fans, doing scenes from Watteau, Fragonard, and Boucher. At twenty he quit this commercial career and began serious study at the studio of Gleyre, where he met a number of his future Impressionist associates.

So many of their works were rejected by the official salon jury that the young men organized their own exhibition in 1874. To this show, Renoir sent the now famous *The Loge* (fig. 71), one of his most beautiful and most typical works. Its appeal lies in the way the painter has portrayed the sense of well-being that radiates from the good-looking well-dressed couple seated in an opera box. We are placed slightly above them and a bit to the side, in what is known as "vantage point perspective." This deliberately unbalanced and spontaneous way of looking at the subject is characteristic of the Impressionist desire to convey an unexpected and casual effect. The notion of the man holding up a glass to his eyes and hiding his face from the spectator was considered quite daring, yet it is a "real" touch as well as a momentarily arrested gesture. He will soon lower his arm and turn to the lady or to the stage; his action will be part of a continuous series of events. It is as though all motion has stopped, enabling the painter to catch a fleeting action.

All these things—the perspective, the quickly seized action, the spontaneity—are part of the Impressionist idea. Compositionally there are other things to note. Renoir has placed these two incompletely seen figures in a tiny space, just as Titian did in his *Venus with a Mirror*. The color shows the effect of the new brilliant color system, especially in the pinks and light blues; but the blacks in the gentleman's dress jacket and the stripes on the lady's gown are those of the Venetian painters, especially Veronese.

The *Oarsmen at Chatou* (color plate XIII) is a characteristic example of Renoir's outdoor painting. He chooses the usual scene of vacationing or picnicking along the Seine or in a little spot in the woods. Young good-looking people (he never shows any other kind) are about to get into the skiff. We are slightly above and to the left. Between us and the distant shore is a continuous shimmer of lavender color that envelopes the entire picture in its atmosphere. It ties together the various parts which otherwise do not show any particular compositional arrangement. The figures stand still, as though bemused, in a typically lyrical and pleasant suspension of action. This is Renoir's particular poetry.

Much as he likes to paint scenes of young people rowing, dining, dancing, or lounging about, his favorite subject is the nude. *Young Woman in the Sun* (fig. 72) is one of dozens of pictures on this theme. It is a vibrant coloristic song of the flesh, frankly sensuous, even pagan, but never sly or underhand. A full round form emerges from the shimmering foliage with immense strength and clarity, with a palpable love of skin and flesh and youthful tender beauty. A century earlier Fragonard had shown a similar feeling for shimmering iridescent movement about his nudes (fig. 48).

Here and in many other pictures, Renoir has brought the

old masters up to date, as it were. He has combined their sense of largeness, their vitality, with his own equally deep feeling for the same kind of beauty and with the color of the modern school.

EDGAR DEGAS

Degas was one of the leading spirits of the Impressionist movement and organized many of its group exhibitions. Nevertheless his paintings differ from the others in a number of important respects. The basis of his training had been fine drawing in the tradition of the old masters. As a result, his approach was entirely distinct from that of the open-air Impressionists. Where they drenched their figures in atmosphere and often lost solidity, he emphasized a tight nervous outline; where they held their figures immobile to build them up in spots of color, he was able to express motion in a direct and exciting way.

The son of a banker, Degas entered the Beaux Arts school where he came under the influence of classical-minded painters. He made copies of many old masters in the Louvre and in Italy, where he favored the Florentine masters, Holbein, and Mantegna. When he returned to Paris, he did a number of group portraits whose formal organization showed his classical training.

In 1862 he turned to scenes of the turf and painted racing subjects. These represent his first venture into the contemporary realism that affected many forward-looking young men at the time. By 1865 Degas had been introduced to the group that met with Édouard Manet at the Café Guerbois, where the talk was all about the new clear painting, the painting of light.

After a term of service in the Franco-Prussian War, Degas came back to Paris. Now began his lifelong series of sub-

jects from the theater and the café. Like the well-known
ballet pictures these were all attempts to depict the most
impermanent action and the most spontaneous effects. To
them were added scenes of people at work, selling hats,
ironing clothes, having their hair combed or nails mani-
cured. These themes are a far cry from the charming oarsmen of Renoir or the smiling landscapes of Monet. The
material chosen by Degas is closest in feeling to the subject
matter of the Realist novel of the nineteenth century and
indeed Degas thought of himself as a sort of sociologist in
paint. Everything was set down in terms of the sharply
angled, momentary technique he soon evolved.

A curious factor in his art is the strange contrast often
found between an ordinary, even ugly scene and the charming color in which it is rendered. His ballet dancers, for example, are not always beautiful. They may be skinny over-
worked little girls straining and puffing to achieve an effect
that will appear in performance as the epitome of grace.
The *Dancers Practicing at the Bar* (fig. 73) is a typical
instance, showing not the glamorous result but the behind-
the-scenes effort. The girls work unself-consciously and
stretch themselves into frequently awkward postures. The
floor has just been watered and the watering can lies at the
left. It is the anchor of a composition that shoots up
diagonally to the right in an exaggerated vantage point perspective. This kind of arrangement in Degas, as in Renoir
and others, stems from Japanese woodcut art introduced to
Europe during the late 1850's. It offered informal subjects
and poses, oblique perspective effects, stylized and outlined
figures, and decorative color contrast.

Degas' painting is often called "keyhole art" for it so
often seems to catch people unawares. But these effects
are consciously sought. Pictures like the *Dancers Practicing
at the Bar* are only partly the result of direct backstage observation. They were actually done by calculated, almost
academic posing of the models in his studio. There the
painter was in complete control of the situation and could
manipulate his figures any way he chose. The horse race

73 DEGAS *Dancers Practicing at the Bar*

scenes are also primarily studio products and, however spontaneous they may appear, the final work was achieved with the aid of wooden horse models.

His bathing scenes, like the pastel drawing *After the Bath* (fig. 74), are not done outdoors as Renoir's so often were. Degas generally shows his women in the tub or nearby it, drying themselves or combing their hair. He actually installed a tub in his studio and made drawings and studies of the models climbing in and out. The high tub offered various stretching possibilities, just as the motions of drying or combing caused the body to bend and curve itself. At the same time a sense of intimacy was conveyed, of witnessing a scene when the subject was unaware. The spectator sees the "house without walls" and looks into a room to observe how people live.

Technically Degas was faced with a conflict between his linear tendencies and an Impressionist feeling for brilliant, dissolving color. His early paintings were uniformly dark, but as he progressed he found it possible to get more brilliance by thinning the paint with liberal doses of turpentine. Finally he dropped oil painting completely for pastel drawing. With colored chalks he was able to draw in linear manner and give color to his figures at the same time. This solution enabled him to keep the forms solid and to make them move, two elements often lacking in orthodox outdoor Impressionism.

Degas provides interesting evidence of the fact that a man may be a political conservative and an artistic progressive. He was a royalist by conviction, but he also took the lead in organizing Impressionist exhibitions. He even helped write the catalogue in which the ideology of the movement is set forth. He remains an outstanding example of this style and one of the greatest artists in the French tradition.

WINSLOW HOMER

WINSLOW HOMER is an American equivalent of the European, Gustave Courbet. Independent of one another they each arrived at similar artistic solutions. Extremely realistic in conception, their painting remains an art of great feeling. Of his own method Homer said, "When I have selected the thing carefully, I paint it exactly as it appears." Thus, in addition to a desire to paint things as they are, the importance of selection and arrangement is also apparent. Homer had a strong sense of design and pattern and an even stronger feeling for the power of the land and the sea. The relation of man to nature appears in his pictures of farmers, fishermen, sailors—men who come into direct and constant contact with her. Courbet too was affected by the majesty of nature and produced a number of powerful sea paintings.

Descendant of an old Yankee family, Homer was brought up in Cambridge, Massachusetts. He spent a good part of his childhood in boating and fishing. With the exception of two years as apprentice to a commercial lithographer, a few classes at the Academy of Design, and some private lessons from a French painter, Homer taught himself by the simple process of painting from life. More than anything else, he was probably helped by a long period of magazine illustrating, for this meant constant application to simple everyday scenes.

His early work in *Harper's Weekly*, like most journalistic illustration of the time, is still rather Victorian. During the

75 HOMER *Rainy Day in Camp*

76 HOMER *Tornado, Bahamas*

Civil War, however, he was sent to the front to cover the human interest side of the conflict. Now a real force and directness emerged. Dealing with the duller side of camp life, the routine tasks, the horseplay and rough jokes of the soldiers, he laid the basis for some of his first important works.

Shortly after the war, Homer did a number of paintings derived from these experiences including *Prisoners from the Front*, and *Rainy Day in Camp* (fig. 75). Here an acute sense of observation is combined with a quiet melancholy. Compositionally, the heavy accents move from the lower left across the picture to the upper right; a lighter diagonal may be traced from the upper left to the lower right. The soldiers gathered about their fire remain the emotional and visual center of the picture, but they are balanced by the rest of camp life.

During the same period he did an elaborate series of genre pictures, his own version of a part of the American scene. He visited various vacation resorts and painted elegant ladies and gentlemen at their sports. These works of the 1870's are somewhat similar to the vacation scenes of the French Impressionists, but they are much more sober in technique. The French pictures are joyous in color and atmospheric in quality. Those of Homer are darkly painted and stress the seriousness of the people involved, even when they are doing something unimportant.

Breezing Up (color plate XIV) shows a monumentality of form that suggests the earlier art of Daumier and Courbet. Frenchmen of this later period, like Renoir and Manet, emphasize the charm of their subjects and the delicate play of light. Homer is more concerned with building up a serious mood and a solid composition. The figures here sit or lie back with a calm solemnity characteristic of Homer's art. The boat swings in curvilinear fashion out of the lower right-hand corner to the upper left, outlining the figures against the sky. This leftward movement is balanced by the figures themselves which move to the right.

His experiences in England in 1881-82 turned Homer,

once and for all, to a study of the sea and its power. In 1884 he settled permanently at Prout's Neck, a lonely spot on the coast of Maine. Except for occasional trips to the north woods or to Florida and the West Indies he remained here for the rest of his life. His deep and abiding love of the sea appears in the many majestic interpretations of her moods. Human beings become less and less important in these works; they are vehicles for his own lonely and austere emotions.

During the winters when he went south, he executed the most famous series of watercolors in the history of American painting. The *Tornado, Bahamas* (fig. 76) represents a constant theme in the work of this period. Under ominous, dark skies the tropical storm comes up without warning to lash the palm trees into a frenzy. The greenish clouds go racing by, and the palm branches bend back to follow. Everything accents the motion to the right: the flat arrangement of the houses, the open shutters, the chimney, the tight little flag whipping in the gale. Homer has undoubtedly been stirred by the sight and has recorded his excitement. Emotive quality has been combined with the careful arrangement of various forms and has created an effective painting.

PAUL CÉZANNE

CÉZANNE is the key figure of the post-Impressionist search for form. In many ways he is the ancestor of both Fauvism and Cubism, the two main streams of twentieth-century French painting.

In the latter part of the nineteenth century, European painting became increasingly experimental. As the artist's market grew smaller, he turned in upon himself, and developed an interest in techniques rather than in subject matter. The Impressionists gave new brilliance to the painter's colors with their semi-scientific color and atmospheric method. But their figures dissolved in a shimmering haze. Toward the end of the century progressive painters like Cézanne tried to correct this deficiency. At the same time, they disavowed the illustrative, story-telling pictures of the academic or conservative school. Apart from the banality of their concern with a pretty sentiment, a homey tale, or ancient allegory, these also lacked form.

The so-called post-Impressionists (Cézanne, Gauguin, Van Gogh, and Seurat) felt this loss of solidity and composition in contemporary painting. Some of them, like Gauguin and Van Gogh, also felt that emotional values had been sacrificed to an either too lyrical or too literal approach.

Cézanne's art marks a self-conscious effort to return to painting the kind of controlled form and space it has not known since the old masters. In the strenuousness of his

77

CÉZANNE

The Card Players

Stephen C. Clark Collection,
New York

attempts he tended to treat his themes more as arrangements of form, color, and texture than as subjects with emotional meaning. The subject matter chosen by the artist had almost always been a direct reflection of his feelings. With Cézanne all this changed; he devoted his life to technique. He tried to make of Impressionism "something as solid and durable as the art of the museums" and neglected the overtly emotional side of painting.

A member of the original Impressionist group, Cézanne soon separated from them. He avoided the atmospheric effects of his associates in favor of a more carefully constructed and arranged composition. Although he used their little spots of clean color, he applied these in such a way that they modulate the form from highlight to shadow. He felt also that the richer the color the more rounded the ultimate form effect would be. Cézanne's most significant contribution, however, came in his treatment of space. In order to get tighter composition, he gradually limited the degree to which the spectator could penetrate the distance. To achieve this, he brought the background as close to the foreground as possible, projecting the forms *toward* the spectator rather than away from him.

In *The Card Players* (fig. 77) each figure is a solid form consisting of clean color areas that move from one intensity to another. The activity of card-playing is subordinated to the composition. The three players are blended into a solid arch balanced by the man at the left and the curtain at the right. The standing man and the curtain, like the pipes on the wall and the converging glances of the players, lead to a central point in the *foreground*. This reverses the usual front-to-back movement of earlier painting. The total effect is to bring the wall close to the table and to move the table itself toward us. This illusion is aided by making the side players touch the upright figure and the curtain, as well as the sides of the picture. Everything is related to the rectangular, front outline of the painting. Yet a picture of this kind, though formal in purpose, is not without emotional

78

CÉZANNE

Mt. Ste. Victoire

*The Phillips Collection,
Washington, D. C.*

meaning. It has a certain seriousness and solemn quietness that bring to mind the great works of the Le Nains in the seventeenth century (fig. 41).

The difference between Cézanne's approach and the outdoor Impressionists' is even more striking in landscape painting. The *Mt. Ste. Victoire* (fig. 78) again shows his ability to organize a theme into a series of controlled and definitely limited elements. The trees at the left and right not only establish the foreground boundaries of the picture, they also relate this foreground area to the mountains in the background. Note, for example how the branches of the tree fit into the curves made by the mountains. Thus the background and the painting as a whole are tilted forward and brought into close relationship with the foreground.

Unlike his predecessors, the artist's aim is not to represent the momentary effect of light striking an object. The post-Impressionist painter like Cézanne or Seurat distributes a permanent, all-over light that has nothing to do with a particular moment in time. In one way this makes the picture less real in the photographic sense; yet the net result is to give a potently solid impression of the individual forms.

Just as the painter arranged the mountain scene, so too has he brought the parts of the *Still Life* (color plate XV) into a patterned relationship. The objects lack the subject relation of the traditional kitchen or living room themes. They have been brought together arbitrarily by the artist to convey the interplay between various kinds of round surfaces. These spread out from the far walls and are brought toward us by the white and flowered cloths. The picture is tilted forward in the typical reverse perspective.

Curiously enough, the persecuted Impressionists had little use for what Cézanne tried to accomplish. As for the public, they lumped Cézanne with the "new painting" and condemned him on the same specious grounds as they did the others. This misanthropic but dedicated man worked in isolation for many years in his home city of Aix. He was "discovered" only shortly before his death. His impact on the modern art world is perhaps greater than that of any other single painter.

PAUL GAUGUIN

THE great seriousness of Cézanne, the escapism of Gauguin, and the passionate rebelliousness of Van Gogh are part of the same pattern. In their various ways the outstanding painters of this period abandon what seem to them the superficial values of nineteenth-century life and art. Cézanne represents the form-seeking side of post-Impressionism; Gauguin and Van Gogh contribute emotional striving and a sense of dissatisfaction with the life of the time.

Gauguin's love of the exotic and strange was deeply rooted. His early childhood had been spent in Peru. The next period of his life, in a Jesuit seminary in France, was very unhappy. At seventeen he shipped as pilot's apprentice on a boat making South American ports. From twenty to twenty-three he was in the French navy as a stoker. He then settled down as a clerk in a stockbroker's office and in the next eleven years made a good deal of money, married, and had five children. The marriage was not altogether successful, due to a restlessness of spirit which led him to art, first as a collector and then as a painter.

From 1880-82 he exhibited with the Impressionists. A year later he gave up a profitable business to devote himself entirely to painting. His wife went back to her family in Copenhagen while Gauguin, trying to make his way in the art world, lived a hand-to-mouth existence as a billboard paster and scenic decorator. In 1886 he had an unsuccessful first show. Gauguin by this time had decided that modern civilization was decadent, so he went off to Brittany where he would not have to contend with the problems of ordinary city life. After a year he came back to Paris, but there was still no recognition. He next went to Martinique where he stayed for a brief period.

Back in Paris once more, he met Van Gogh and his picture-dealer brother Theo. For a few months he lived with the former at Arles in the south of France. This short-lived and disastrous experience ended in Van Gogh's first nervous breakdown. Again Gauguin tried "unspoiled" Brittany where the peasants lived as they had for centuries. Here he took a leading part in the so-called Pont-Aven school of painting.

Under the influence of the profound piety of the Breton people and the angular forms of their native religious art, he produced a number of pictures that represent a departure from the Impressionist viewpoint. Although brightly charged with color, a painting like *The Yellow Christ* (fig. 79) has an altogether new and symbolic quality. It conveys the solemn contemplative frame of mind of people who have just come from church and carry in their minds the thoughts evoked by the sermon. Thus the women in their peasant costumes sit about the foot of a Cross conjured up out of their imaginations. This is quite different from the saccharine superficiality with which academic painters so often treat religious themes.

The form also differs from both the conventional photographic stories of the academicians and the shimmering Impressionist pictures. Instead of a detailed illustration, the artist causes the unrealistic, yellow Christ to emerge from the simplified forms of the women about the Cross. It is a frankly imaginary or spiritual scene; not a Crucifixion as such, but an image, a dream of a Crucifixion. The broad color areas recall medieval enamels or stained glass, while the figure of Christ is derived from sculptures of the Middle Ages. The perspective suggests the arrangements of Japanese art, already seen in Impressionist painting, with the spectator high up and to the side, looking through a number of prominent foreground objects to the space beyond.

79 GAUGUIN *The Yellow Christ*

As in Cézanne the space has a deliberately restricted quality. The patterning of trees, hills, and other forms does not lead *back* into the painting. Rather the eye moves back and forth *across* the surface. The yellow of the Christ is repeated in the hills; the blue of the women's clothes in the sky and horizon; the foreground green in similar accents higher up and further back. The total effect is a vertically projected pattern of pleasant curving color areas, always related to something in the foreground. It is what Gauguin calls Synthetism, the synthetic or artificial reconstruction of landscape, still life, or whatever interests the artist.

His later pictures were of Tahiti, where he finally went to escape from European civilization. Though often less symbolic than *The Yellow Christ*, these works share the same qualities. In the *Barbaric Tales* (fig. 80), as before, Gauguin is interested in the independent and non-naturalistic function of color. Strongly intensified and covering a broad area, color has a new power and meaning. This is heightened by the sinuous movement of linear contours which represent the process of growth itself. Figures are not only abstracted, they are integrated into the picture pattern. They become a symbolic part of nature and its inherent growth. Gauguin's frequent theme of women outdoors is also favored by the Fauves and Expressionists of the next generation.

In the search for a means to express his feeling for "primitive" existence, Gauguin combines the linear art brought from France with Buddhist-Indian, Egyptian, and other Eastern art forms that are highly civilized, however "different." The woman facing us in this picture is posed like a Buddha, legs crossed and hand pointing to the ground, "calling upon the Earth to witness." Here in this broadly colored, sinuously contoured, and formally controlled picture, Gauguin sums up his protest against modern materialism—his own version of the return to nature.

VINCENT VAN GOGH

Van gogh's life is not merely the story of an individual's personal misfortune. It is a symbol of the intelligent man's refusal to accept the hypocrisy and injustice of nineteenth-century materialistic society. Like his contemporaries in many parts of the world, he put into pictorial form this great dissatisfaction. The degree to which he was unable to cope with worldly existence is a visible sign of the tragedy of modern man.

The son of a Dutch minister, Van Gogh came to painting through relatives in the art business. At the age of fifteen he was given a job in The Hague branch of the family firm, Goupil and Co., but did not like the work. He was shifted to London in 1873 where he suffered intensely from the refusal of his landlady's daughter to marry him. For some years he shuttled back and forth between the various branches of the company. Nowhere was he able to accommodate himself to what he considered the dishonesty of telling people that the pictures he was selling were good art.

His natural religious tendencies led him to try the ministry, but he failed to qualify and volunteered to do missionary and relief work instead. Characteristically he chose the most miserable industrial area in northern Europe, the Belgian *Borinage*. He lived with the coal miners, shared their miserable lives, and worked with such fervor that the officials in Brussels dismissed him. In these wretched sur-

81

VAN GOGH
The Night Café

Stephen C. Clark
Collection, New York

roundings he began to draw sketches of the miners and their families. From there he went to Brussels to study art, developing very slowly.

A second disappointment in love was followed by a period in The Hague where Van Gogh studied with his cousin, the animal painter Anton Mauve. In 1884 at the home of his parents he produced a second batch of studies —soapy-green spiritualized sketches dealing with the lives of the poor peasants and weavers of that place. Although crude and awkward in many ways, these early works, such as the famous *Potato Eaters*, show a moving and impressive intensity of feeling for people.

In 1886 his brother Theo, who had become an important art dealer, brought him to Paris. He met Degas, Seurat, Gauguin, Lautrec, and others and fell under the influence of Impressionist color and Japanese perspective effects. But the excitement of the big city was not good for him; in 1888 he was sent to Arles in the south of France for his health.

Van Gogh's art had changed from the dark tones of his early work to the more joyous hues of Impressionism. Now under the powerful southern sun his colors intensified tremendously. Varying the Impressionist technique, he applied his spots of paint in a systematic personal manner. Tiny wriggles of pure pigment were squeezed out of the tube directly onto the canvas. His *La Mousmé* (color plate XVI) utilizes this trick of color application; through it the picture is set in motion in a new way. The emphasis now is on sinuous curving movements, on outlines of form as in Gauguin, but sparkling and vibrant in effect rather than broad and resonant. The slight clashes of color create a restless reaction, as do the rough and irregular outlines. Comparing this girl's expression to that of Renoir's young women, we see the difference between the joyousness of Impressionism and what Van Gogh called "the heartbroken expression of our time."

Superficial charm and surface description are the furthest

82 VAN GOGH *Cypresses*

things from the painter's mind. He distorts the various elements of the figure and makes them conform to the outline of the chair; the body is reduced to a series of color and form patterns. Thus he allows us to look at the face against the pale background, giving an internal rather than external quality. Instead of a description or "impression" of form and atmosphere, Van Gogh is concerned with an "expression" of the inner character of the person or the scene.

The Night Café (fig. 81) is a locale treated many times before by other artists. But most painters use the café as a scene of enjoyment, whereas Van Gogh brings together a group of unhappy beings who have no other place to make love, like the figures at the background left, or even to sleep like the unfortunates with their heads on the tables. It becomes a scene of social misery; the sad little people scattered about the room are to be pitied. The deliberately clashing reds and greens, violets and blues (that were bland, harmonious combinations in the hands of Impressionists) are Van Gogh's way of giving greater impact to the scene. It is "a place where one can ruin oneself, run mad or commit a crime."

Van Gogh's treatment of nature stands in the same violent contrast to the pleasant and charming scenes of the Impressionists. In the *Cypresses* (fig. 82) Renoir's small spots of pure color are elongated into agitated and wriggling little forms, each with a life of its own; each adding to the total impact of restlessness and unhappiness. The painter stands close to the tree watching it move, exaggerating its gentle curves into heaving tumultuous outlines that express both the force of the southern mistral winds and the very process of growth. By cutting off the sides of the composition he forces us into his own compressed and intense mood, hinting at immense distances rather than showing them.

The twisting flamelike movements of the trees as they rush skyward, the broad sweeping linear curve of the violet hill coming in from the right, the swirling clouds in the sky are fragments of the vastness of nature. They have been arrested here for a brief instant of emotional tension which engulfs the spectator as it did the painter himself.

HENRI MATISSE

THE crisis implicit in post-Impressionism became sharper by the turn of the century and in the years immediately preceding World War I. During this period painters no longer reflected the state of the world in the direct terms used by men like Delacroix. After a long period of isolation and public nonacceptance, modern art turned to experimental and technical practices. Thus the response of artists to events was indirect and abstract rather than socially useful in the old sense. Yet the painters and other creative persons of the early twentieth century were aware of the mounting political tensions. Before the first World War actually broke out they provided clear evidence of the imminent destruction.

Modern art in the first decade of this century was an extension and intensification of trends already evident in the works of Cézanne, Van Gogh and Gauguin. French art maintained its traditional formal bent, but on a more abstract level. The various elements were exaggerated in keeping with the spiritual needs of the new era. The post-Impressionists (except Van Gogh) held reality under control. The greater dynamism of this period results in Fauvist coloristic exaggeration, Cubist fragmentation of form, Futurist glorification of the machine, and similar expressions of the artist's reaction to the times.

The first important group of the period was called the Fauve or "wild beasts" by the critics. It was formally organized in 1905 under the leadership of Henri Matisse and

Courtesy of Mr. and Mrs. Leigh B. Block, Chicago

New Museum of Modern Western Art, Moscow

included Derain, Vlaminck, Rouault and Dufy. Like most painters early in the century, they were influenced by Cézanne, Van Gogh, and Gauguin.

From Cézanne, Matisse and others derived their interest in color as a form-building device. The earlier painter controlled his space and limited it; the newer painters were even more severe. They confined the figure to an arbitrarily restricted space which required a new kind of movement. This movement was found in the expressive contours and large bold color areas of Gauguin, as well as the short sharp color strokes of Van Gogh. These set the figure in motion with a curvilinear side-to-side and up-and-down action while the form itself constantly vibrates.

The Young Sailor (fig. 83) is one of Matisse's early works. Its brutal simplification of outline is different from the smoothness of Gauguin to the degree that Matisse makes use of other sources, notably the ceramic and manuscript art of Persia. Yet the lavender background of the picture and the large sections of bright color come directly from Gauguin. In the earlier artist, however, the color areas were suavely harmonious. Here, there is a deliberate discord in the brilliant blue of the shirt and sharp green of the trousers. This, like the short abrupt color strokes, brings to mind the expressive methods of Van Gogh.

Although Cézanne's modeling qualities are reflected here, Matisse is more concerned with a series of curvilinear arrangements. These movements gradually lead the eye from the top down and carry the relationship of greens, blues, and other colors from one part of the picture to the other. Works of this kind deviate from physical reality and become arrangements of form and color for their own sake. Nevertheless there is still a strong and meaningful expression in the accentuated green staring eyes, the red and green lips, and the shadows under the cap.

In *The Dessert* (fig. 84) Matisse again subordinates reality to an artistic arrangement of form and color patterns. Although there is a specific subject—a woman placing fruits about a table—the emphasis is on the balance of rectangular and rounded forms (the straightness of the former accentuating the rhythmic curves of the latter) and on the careful placement of related color accents in various parts of the picture. The significance of the woman's activity or her personal involvements disappear before the joyous play of forms and colors.

Matisse's woman is a curved accent balanced by the rectangular area of the chair opposite. The squareness of the window is relieved by the formalized trees in the background (compare with the trees of Gauguin, fig. 79), while the severity of the table alternates with the curved bottles, fruit, and patterns that cover it. These patterns, repeated in the wall and trees, give the picture its all-over flat movement and help to maintain the controlled two-dimensional quality. In the achievement of such a textured and brilliantly colored surface, Matisse took advantage of the decorative sophisticated art of the Near East which offers similar vivid effects in its pottery, manuscripts, and textiles.

In pictures of this sort the subject is a mere pretext for artistic manipulation of form, color, space, and texture. What is important is not the so-called reality of a given situation or theme, but rather the artist's "form reaction" to what he has chosen to depict. This may be regarded as a denial of everyday reality. But it is the artist's own kind of reality, the world of aesthetic relationships in which he chooses to move.

PABLO PICASSO

Picasso is unquestionably the outstanding figure of this century in painting. His influence is so wide, his creative variety so far-reaching that he has had an incalculable effect on the course of modern art. The most significant of his achievements are: first, the development (with Georges Braque) of a so-called Cubist method of looking at things; and second, the powerfully expressive applications of this method in the period after the first World War.

Unlike many modern masters to whom technique is far more important than content, Picasso has a constant strong undercurrent of feeling that lends his work a distinct quality. His primary concern is with form problems—indeed, Picasso provides the most significant extension of the Cézanne approach. But whether for personal reasons or because of his Spanish background, his art continually asserts a potent emotional element.

Picasso arrived in Paris in 1901. His early work in France combined the spiritual qualities of El Greco with the disillusion of Lautrec. The pathetic blue clowns, actors, poor people, and musicians are his direct expression of the sadness of the period.

During the first decade of the century there were large-scale exhibitions of Van Gogh, Gauguin, and Cézanne. Although all artists of the period were affected by Cézanne, Matisse and his Fauve followers leaned toward the decorative and expressive qualities of Gauguin and Van Gogh; Picasso on the other hand, began with an unmistakable interest in the formal compositions and geometrical effects of Cézanne.

At the home of Gertrude Stein he met Matisse who introduced him to the new vogue for African sculpture. This art appealed to many younger men who were somewhat jaded and bored with civilized society and its sophisticated forms. For them the direct and powerful violence of the primitive sculptors had an immediate attraction. It was regarded as a healthful and strengthening influence. But for painters like Picasso and Braque, African art had other virtues as well. It brought a simplification that reduced form to sharp, angular, diamondlike facets—from which the term "Cubism" was derived. The fiercely simplified African figures also gave a new sense of movement to the works of Picasso. Combined with the rigid compositional schemes of Cézanne, these faceted forms imparted an incessant back-and-forth quality to the picture space.

In this new kind of picture and new way of looking at things, Picasso offered two special factors. *The Three Musicians* (fig. 85) showed, first, an interpenetration of the figures and background. There is less and less distinction between the objects themselves and the space in which they are set. This aesthetic rather than everyday reality is similar to that achieved by Matisse, although here the emphasis is on angular and geometrically shaped forms.

Second and more important, these figures are viewed by the painter in an entirely new way. He has, so to speak, walked about the three men, seeing them from all sides simultaneously—rather than from the traditional frontal position. From this round-and-round kaleidoscopic vista, the painter has selected a series of fragmentary views (or perspective boxes). He has chosen parts of the figures that lend themselves to arrangement. These he has deliberately reconstructed into a design of front, back, and side fragments that together offer a decorative and dynamic pattern, colored strikingly and effectively.

Comparing this abstraction with *The Dessert* of Matisse (fig. 84), we find that the latter depends on charming sim-

85 PICASSO *The Three Musicians* Courtesy of The Philadelphia Museum of Art

86 PICASSO *Guernica*

The Museum of Modern Art, New York

plification of form and its subordination to an all-over color and texture pattern. Picasso's method is far more dynamic, for it begins with the destruction or "visual explosion" of the figure. From the fragments he purposely selects appropriate pieces to re-create an original and more active form. The net result is a constantly moving series of angular parts across a surface and, to a limited extent, into a space.

The consequence of this approach to form was a further breaking away from the everyday and the expected in art. It was naturally greeted with indignation by conventional critics. Its development, however, has led to a host of allied movements such as Futurism, Rayonism, de Stijl, Machine art, Purism, and the streamlined effects found in modern industrial design. All these things are related more or less directly to the ideas evolved by Picasso, Braque, and their colleagues in the years before the first World War.

Picasso himself has since gone on with numerous variants of the Cubist approach. He turns here and there to decorative adaptations of the method or imbues his fragmented forms with powerful feeling. The mixture of Cubist distortion and violent emotion is perhaps nowhere as forceful and expressive as in the famous *Guernica* (fig. 86) of 1937. This work on the Spanish civil war has often been compared with Goya's portrayals of the disasters of war in his time (see fig. 58). Entirely different in form, it has the same intense feeling of man's inhumanity to man, the same bitter anger at the slaughter of a civilian population.

Picasso's destruction of form, which in the early years of the century had anticipated the violence of World War I, is applied here to a similar purpose. The dead and mangled forms lying at the base of the stark black and white picture, the agony of the dying figure at the right, the suffering of the mother lamenting her dead child, the tortured form of the horse, are all evidence of his blazing indignation at what the bombers of Hitler and Mussolini had done to his country.

Forms penetrate forms, views overlap views, background and foreground mingle in this charnel house lit by the frightening light overhead. The figure of the bull in the upper left is a symbol of fascist brutality, the horse represents the wounded country; the shieking figure that brings the oil lamp to illuminate these horrors is the conscience of mankind. Even for those unfamiliar with Picasso's method, the sheer horror and violence of this scene are unforgettable reminders of the meaning of war.

MARC CHAGALL

THE art of Marc Chagall provides evidence of the ever-increasing modern interest in the play of the subconscious mind. The exposure of the thoughts that lie just below the level of consciousness developed, during the 1920's, into the movement known as Surrealism. But even in the pre-World War I years, Chagall was already deeply involved with this kind of expression. His art illustrates the fruitfulness of Cubism which, early in the century, was absorbed by many different types of artists. In Chagall's case, the faceted forms and overlapping views were combined with wonderfully rich color and an equally powerful imaginative feeling. This more fanciful and coloristic Cubism is considerably different from either the formal or the decorative applications of the Cubist method so widely followed after the war.

Chagall's background was that of the small Russian-Jewish village. In the town of Vitebsk he absorbed vivid impressions of the picturesque architecture and the poignant feelings of the old world legends and religion of his forefathers. His artistic career began with a period spent in the school of the scenic designer Leon Bakst in St. Petersburg. Like most Europeans interested in modern art, Chagall was attracted to Paris where he lived from 1911 to 1914.

He arrived in France at the high point of Fauve coloristic development and Cubist formal fragmentation. His own inclination was toward the vivid color schemes of his background and of Bakst. These strong red and green tonalities

87   CHAGALL   *I and My Village*

were now combined with Cubist overlapping views, which other painters were already making more colorful. Chagall himself contributed to this mixture the elements of fantasy and unexpectedness. His subjects from the subconscious mind might emerge in dreams or imaginative revery.

I and My Village (fig. 87), painted in Paris during 1911, is one of those blendings of the real and the unreal that give to Chagall his important place in the history of early Surrealist painting. The background shows the gables and towers of the typical little Russian village of the artist's memory. The church at the left has an oversize head staring out; the two center houses are upside down. A peasant walks along with a scythe over his shoulder, while a woman proceeds unconcernedly on her head.

This fanciful attitude is also shown in the two large heads of a peasant and a cow which confront each other. The green and white faceted peasant offers a bit of foliage to the white and blue animal with its overlapping areas. The picture of a woman milking is placed as an overlay on the head of the cow. The quizzical look on the face of this animal, the humorous simplicity of the farmer, the joyous exuberance of the general color scheme give paintings of this type their unusually poetic and charming quality.

Chagall's combination of the real and unreal (the essence of the later Surrealist method) is different from that of Dali and others. He does not mask sadistic, sexual, or other "forbidden" meanings. His art is straightforwardly sensual when that response is called for; otherwise it is colorful, gay, imaginative, and poetic. It evokes images from the painter's childhood, his readings, and other experiences that have been absorbed into his subconscious.

When war broke out, Chagall returned to his native Russia. During 1915–16, before he went into the army, he painted a series of specifically Jewish subjects including weddings and rabbis. Some were based on vicious pogroms he had witnessed. Others were fanciful as before, but now pervaded by an increasing melancholy caused by the times themselves as much as by his self-conscious Jewishness.

88

CHAGALL
Over Vitebsk

Private Collection

Over Vitebsk (fig. 88) is an instance of this sort of painting. There is still faceting of certain portions, such as the snow-covered foreground and the houses at the upper right which have an angular quality and a melancholy poetry. Above this strange road with its forbidding church, a quiet dark figure floats. It is an old Jew with a pack on his back, the traditional wandering peddler who symbolizes the insecurity of his race and its enforced economic function in the old world.

Amid the sharp details of the picture and its sense of frightening reality, the flying figure of the old man comes as a kind of shock. It supplies the unreal component in the real-unreal effects often met in dreams. There, as here, an obviously impossible element may be made believable by its existence among so many true and clearly seen things. In other pictures Chagall makes the combination more humorous than in this rather sad story—especially when he celebrates his own life and his love for his wife.

After the outbreak of the Russian Revolution, Chagall returned to Vitebsk to direct its art school during 1917–18. A disagreement with the authorities over how poetic and fanciful he could be drove him to Moscow where he became art director for the Academic Jewish Theatre. In 1921 he was still in Moscow working for Stanislavsky's Art Theatre as a scenic designer. But a shift in official policy condemned modern art as a "bourgeois luxury" and Chagall departed finally from his native land. From 1922 until the Nazi invasion of 1940 he lived in Paris. He returned there after the war and still lends his artistic authority to the imaginative and poetic painting that is his real contribution to modern art.

OSKAR KOKOSCHKA

EXPRESSIONISM is another early twentieth-century reaction to the unhappiness of modern times. The movement began in Germany and Austria at the same time as Fauvism and Cubism began in France; but it is far less interested in orderly form. Instead it is imbued with the mysticism, romanticism, and powerful emotion associated with the Germanic tradition.

Expressionist painters like Kokoschka are impelled toward the portrayal of spiritual disturbance. To achieve this end they turn in upon themselves, distorting surface reality to find the truth that lies beneath it. The differences between the systematic French artists and the more emotive Austro-Germans may stem from the fact that the western European nations had become further democratized by the late nineteenth century. In central Europe, on the other hand, medievalism, militarism, and an authoritarian way of life were dominant until the first World War. In church, school, family, the army, and civil service, there was strong regimentation and suppression of individual liberty.

For some, this situation may have been quite acceptable, but it did not meet the spiritual needs of many artists and other intellectuals. They fought back in the frenzied upsurge known as Expressionism. These painters and writers did not react to the strains of the period, the threat of war, and the added weight of Austro-German authoritarianism in the logical manner of the Fauves and Cubists. They offered a far more taut and contorted response. Theirs was

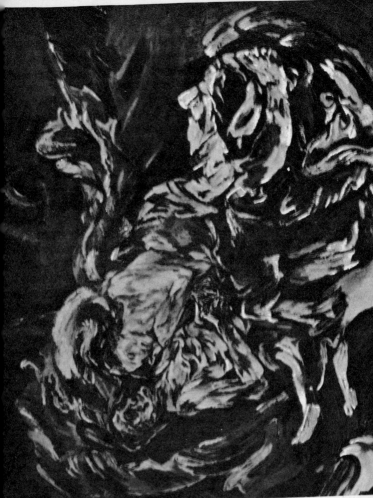

89

KOKOSCHKA
Tempest

*Courtesy of the
Kunstmuseum, Basle*

90

KOKOSCHKA
Lake Geneva

*Paul Geier
Collection,
Cincinnati*

a frantic destruction of the physical world, an attempt to release themselves from an unpleasant environment by losing themselves in the infinite. Through the alteration of form, color, and space of reality, they arrived at a statement of their violent unhappiness.

Expressionist painters may be divided into two broad classes: those who deal with recognizable (however distorted) forms and those who lean toward the abstract and nonobjective. In the first group are artists like Oskar Kokoschka and Ernst Ludwig Kirchner; in the second are Wassily Kandinsky, Paul Klee, Franz Marc, and others.

The Austrian-born Kokoschka was trained in the Vienna Arts and Crafts School. From the beginning he had been attracted by museum collections of primitive African and Oceanic art, just as his French contemporaries had been. The latter used this material for compositional or decorative purposes. Kokoschka found in it a source of violence and power that was close to his own desire "to create around me a world of my own in which I could survive the progressive disruption going on all over the world." His first efforts were attacked for their unconventionality; he was soon looked upon as "a public terror" and dismissed from his school. In 1909 the works he sent to the official show and the two violently unconventional plays he presented caused a serious scandal and he decided to leave the country.

After a short period in Switzerland, Kokoschka went to Germany where the way had already been prepared by the Dresden painters of 1905 organized as *Die Brücke* (The Bridge). His arrival in Berlin did a good deal to stimulate the German movement and also furthered his own development. By 1914, he was an important figure. In those years before the outbreak of war, some of his most powerful works were done.

Perhaps the best known of these is the *Tempest* (fig. 89) whose flickering all-over mysterious light and mystic feeling suggest the art of El Greco. Kokoschka begins with a simple concrete theme—himself and his sweetheart.

Through powerful twisting of form and alteration of color, through projection of the two figures into an unreal world of the spirit, he conveys the unique quality of his art. On this unworldly plane, the painter and his love whirl through space, carried by emotion rather than by any real force. By deliberately moving away from reality in every aspect of this work, the artist forces us to concentrate on its spiritual quality.

His painting of nature is similarly "internal" rather than "external." *Lake Geneva* (fig. 90) of 1924 is comparable to the conceptions of Van Gogh (one of the greatest influences on the Expressionist movement). Like the earlier painter's efforts, it is a somber and tragic projection of the artist's own feelings. The actual color and form of the various items are distorted to arrive at the true essence of this section of nature. Kokoschka strives for emotional and philosophical meaning rather than purely physical appearance. The mountains and peaks of Switzerland exercised a constant fascination on Germanic painters and writers; they responded violently to the endlessness and power of the great crags to which they were perhaps drawn by some intellectual claustrophobia.

Profound figure studies have also been made by Kokoschka. Especially in those of his early life, he probed deeply into the nature of each subject and brought to the surface the inner character of the individual.

Kokoschka has remained a fighter against spiritual and political repression. Driven out of Germany by the Nazis, he kept on the move for many years, changing his residence as Hitler's armies overflowed Europe. Since 1938 he has been living in London. Many works done during this period were conscious and forceful anti-fascist statements. One of the most significant artists of the twentieth century, Kokoschka has also contributed magnificently to the intellectual morality of our time.

WASSILY KANDINSKY

KANDINSKY is one of those key figures in the modern movement whose ideas have influenced a whole generation of artists. His works have been augmented considerably by theoretical writings like *Concerning the Spiritual in Art*. He is important as a representative of abstract Expressionism and as the first modern painter to divorce himself entirely from subject matter.

The form of Expressionism found in Kokoschka means a deliberately violent outpouring of emotion. The other side of the movement, however, is more spontaneous and impulsive, more poetic and sensitive. It is genuinely lyrical and even musical. This is represented by the art of Kandinsky and his Munich *Blue Rider* colleagues: Franz Marc, Paul Klee, and others. Theirs is an attempt to destroy form in order to arrive at the reality beneath it. Through the interpenetrating facets of Cubism, they attempt to lose themselves in the vastness of nature, the immensity of the universe, and the general mystery of existence. In their highly developed intuitive response to life, they may try to feel themselves into the existence of other beings such as animals, children or peasants. This is an evidence of the nonrational, mystical, and other-worldly quality which turns them to abstractions rather than to real forms.

For Kandinsky, and other *Blue Rider* artists, a color may represent a distinct idea (the inheritance of Gauguin and the Fauves). For some of them, color and line have a specific musical quality as well. By comparison with the art of Kokoschka, works like Kandinsky's are more spiritual and dematerialized, less and less tied to the world of matter.

Kandinsky was born in Moscow in 1866 and at the age of eighteen took up law and economics. He was offered a teaching job at a university but decided to study painting and went to Munich in Germany. There this highly intellectual Russian, with his own variant of that country's mysticism, plunged into the seething excitement of the modern movement at the beginning of the century. He traveled about and visited Paris at the time of the earliest Fauve and Cubist developments, but responded slowly to these new stimuli. His art was still under the influence of the twisting linear decorative "youth style," derived largely from Van Gogh, and the broad symbolic color effects of Gauguin.

There was a rapid development, however, and by 1910 he had written his influential book *Concerning the Spiritual in Art*. A year later he and his Munich colleagues organized themselves as *The Blue Rider*. From this point on his paintings moved increasingly toward nonobjectivity— the abandonment of subject matter in the old sense. The well known *Improvisation No. 30* (fig. 91) shows the transition from pictures with specific subjects to the purely abstract and musical viewpoint that was soon to dominate. Already recognizably real objects have been cut down to a minimum. It is, as the title implies, one of a series of improvisations on form and color areas. Because of the reduction of subject matter, the painter can concern himself with his own spontaneous and almost automatic responses.

He refers to this picture as Cannons but says:

> "The designation 'Cannons' is not to be conceived as indicating the 'contents' of the picture. These contents are indeed what the spectator *lives* or *feels* while under the effect of the *form and color combinations* of the

91 KANDINSKY *Improvisation No. 30*

92   KANDINSKY   *Little Circles, No. 555. 1935*

picture. . . . The presence of the cannons . . . could probably by explained by the constant war talk that had been going on throughout the year. . . .

"The observer must learn to look at the picture as a graphic representation of a *mood* and not as a representation of *objects*."

This points the way toward a complete break with subject matter. In the improvisations, free forms and colors play across the surface of the canvas in lyrical and musical fashion. Here the painter improvises with forms, lines, and colors much as a composer might with musical tones and rhythms.

With the outbreak of the war·in 1914, Kandinsky returned to Russia. After the Revolution he occupied various posts under the young Soviet government, serving as teacher, organizer of museums, and art educator. By 1919 his free, flowing style had become more geometric, under the influence of the Cubist-inspired Russian Constructivists. Although the work of this group was rather dry, unemotional, and mechanical, their strong form quality attracted Kandinsky.

Added to his own feeling for spontaneous and even humorous expression this geometric interest produced the effects as seen in the watercolor painting *Little Circles* (fig. 92). Here the forms are balls, ovals, and rectangles which have been softened in effect by a free movement carried joyously over the composition. One may perhaps think of planetary phenomena, but only in the most general way, since the little balls do not refer to any specific objects but to shapes in motion.

Kandinsky returned to Germany in 1922 as a teacher at the newly organized *Bauhaus*, and was connected with this famous industrial art school until its dissolution by the Nazis in 1933. He then lived in Paris until his death in 1944.

More than any other modern painter, Kandinsky has shown the great musical possibilities of subjectless painting. Both his relatively amorphous early works and the more strictly formed later pictures have had a tremendous impact on modern art. In the United States a whole school of Abstract Expressionists owes much to his example.

MAX BECKMANN

Beckmann is part of the generation that developed in a bitter and disillusioned Germany after the first World War. But his importance as a creative artist went far beyond the misery of that period and produced a highly personal and emotive kind of expression. No other modern painter has insisted with such constant and moving force on the value of the individual human being. This has been conveyed through a unique symbolism, as significant as that of Picasso, Chagall, Orozco, and other modern masters. Although quite different in form from his fellow-Expressionist Kokoschka, there is in him the same probing of the soul, the same ceaseless indictment of injustice, cruelty, and sham.

The son of a well-to-do flour merchant, Beckmann began to draw when he was a child. In 1900 he left school to enter the conservative Weimar Academy. There he was influenced by the nineteenth-century idealist painter Hans von Marées, whose monumental symbolic forms left a permanent mark on his art. During his early travels he was impressed by the human sympathy of Rembrandt, and the statuesque power and space composition of Piero della Francesca.

In 1905 he went to Berlin, which was seething with its first efforts to create a modern art. Impressionism and post-Impressionism had just been heard of. Beckmann combined these new trends with his own inclination for emotionally expressive, monumental figures. His version of Impressionist art is Germanic as well as personal. It is solid, unconcerned with atmospheric effects, and lends greater importance to the subject. This was Beckmann until the outbreak of the first World War, in which he served as a medical orderly.

The scenes he witnessed in the course of duty and his own two-year illness gave his art an entirely new direction. He not only turned to scenes of horror and suffering but evolved a special style for handling such material. Like other artists faced with a particular aesthetic need, he studied past efforts to cope with very similar problems. In his case it was the art of the Middle Ages with its accent on suffering and its expressive emotionality.

The famous *Family Picture* (fig. 93) shows how Beckmann profited from his adaptations of medieval form and feeling. The sculpturesque and isolated figures, the seriousness, the deliberate distortions of form and space, all suggest the older art. The composition is arranged two-dimensionally across a shallow surface as in the Flemish *Descent from the Cross* (fig. 11). Here also the arrangement suggests sculptured figures set in a broad niche. The figures themselves are unusually tall in proportion to the space to achieve greater emotional expressiveness.

The background is brought into close relationship with the foreground through such details as the right-hand door that moves toward the front picture line and the ceiling that carries the eye inward. Similarly the piano lid connects the back wall and the front of the room, as does the young woman fixing her hair at the left. The artist in his search for a controlled space makes as many objects as possible refer to either the top, sides, or bottom of the two-dimensional picture frame.

The figures have deliberately been fitted into a tight space much too small and too narrow to hold them. This gives a certain tension and conveys the sense of repression so strongly felt by the artist. As in medieval art, the heads are too large for the bodies, adding an intensity which is

93 BECKMANN *Family Picture*

94
BECKMANN
Christ in Limbo

augmented by the seriousness of their poses and their self-contained expressions.

Beckmann tried to express here a kind of cold hopelessness. The feeling of being hemmed in and unable to do anything about it characterizes the Germany of the 1920's, when everything went up in the smoke of inflation and social disorder. An ordinary family scene (compare Le Nain, fig. 41, or Vermeer, fig. 42) turns out to be a room with too many people, whose expressions show varying degrees of futility and despair.

During the 1930's and 40's he developed a monumental and personal figure style, quite different from the previous rather medieval forms. He was increasingly concerned with expressive coloristic art and philosophical significance. These elements are brought together more graphically in the somber and majestic *Christ in Limbo* (fig. 94).

The austere and impressive figure of Christ is distorted in the peculiarly tense manner that is Beckmann's own. He stands with the majestic severity of some ancient Oriental god, the crown of thorns on His head, His wounded hand raised in a simple gesture. Balancing the powerful emblem of Good is the monster which represents the devil. This imaginatively horrible and demonic conception of the Evil One is not traditional in Christian art, but is by no means unusual as a Germanic conception.

Here is no theological quarrel between Good and Evil. For Beckmann these problems did not exist in that form. His paintings were always meant to express some philosophic or humanistic idea. Thus the Christ bears a candle to bring light to mankind and to drive away the man with the sword, the brutal pitiless symbol of war.

Beckmann lived through the first World War, the growing menace of Nazism from which he barely escaped, and the terror of life in occupied Holland during the second World War; his last years were spent in the United States. His poetic and tragic representations of man's fate were an inevitable reaction to the events of our time.

JOSÉ CLEMENTE OROZCO

For four centuries Mexico labored under the burden of a medieval agrarian system inherited from the Spanish conquest. Although the break from the mother country occurred in 1810, the system itself did not begin to disappear until the Revolution of 1910. This brought with it the modern Mexican cultural renaissance and the great paintings of Orozco.

After ten years of bloodshed, Mexico settled down in 1920 to build a new life. This dream of social improvement included public education on a hitherto unknown scale. Part of the program was an art for the people. The Mexican government furnished walls for mural painters and subsistence wages that enabled them to decorate a number of public buildings. From the large group of idealistic painters involved in the early program, three emerged as leaders: Orozco, Rivera, and Siqueiros.

The first period of this renaissance was short-lived. As the social revolution suffered its first set-back, the painting of revolutionary murals was temporarily shelved. From 1924–34, production in Mexico fell off sharply and the most important works were done by artists in self-imposed exile. Orozco did murals at Pomona College in California, the New School in New York, and Dartmouth College in New Hampshire; Rivera painted in San Francisco, Detroit, and New York; Siqueiros worked in Los Angeles and Buenos Aires.

96 OROZCO *Hidalgo y Costilla*

In 1934 with the advent of President Cárdenas the Mexican mural movement revived. Its most significant works were those produced by Orozco in his native city of Guadalajara. There between 1936 and 1939 he created a number of frescoes which are among his undoubted masterpieces: the works in the university, the decorations in the Government Palace, and those in the Cabañas Orphanage.

Orozco had lived through the years of the Revolution in Mexico. He participated as a war artist under Carranza and witnessed much bloodshed and carnage. To him and to his contemporaries the Revolution was a very real thing. But the personality of Orozco with its compassionate mystical approach, its flaming righteous indignation at the sufferings of his people, gives his art its special character.

In the auditorium of the University of Guadalajara he first painted the dome with a group of serene figures representing *Creative Man*. Below these, on the back wall and two side panels of the stage, he projected an allegory of humanity tortured and misled by demagogues. On one part of the back wall, he shows these greedy well-fed leaders with their books from which appropriate but insincere phrases are quoted to stay the dissatisfaction of the masses. On the rest of the wall, the starved and beaten arise from the flames of their torment. In the dynamic power of this scene, the second group flows irresistibly against the first, with the force of emotional exaltation.

The side panels of the stage show something of the tremendous psychological power and expressionistic agony that give Orozco's work its characteristic intensity. The right-hand panel, sometimes called *The Victims* (fig. 95), has three gaunt emaciated forms—one standing, one kneeling, and the third, a child, lying on the ground. These are Mexico's poor, the miserable ones for whom Orozco felt a great and constant compassion. The forms are flat and graphic rather than sculpturesque. The linear outlines of the figures lead the eye to follow the shape of the arc.

Flickering light and dark highlights suggest the magical light of El Greco, as do the elongated and distorted forms.

They are dematerialized and spiritual rather than material substance. Yet these figures are no more "unreal" than are the figures of Kokoschka and other Expressionists. Like them, Orozco has begun with a concrete situation, but has not limited himself to a bald statement of objective fact. Through exaggerations of form and color, he has portrayed the emotional and spiritual essence of the situation.

At the Government Palace in Guadalajara, Orozco decorated the main staircase with a mural on the theme of the Mexican Revolution. On the left-hand wall of the stairwell is the story of *The Religious Phantasms in Alliance with Militarism*, Orozco's conception of two Mexican despotisms. Opposite this symbolic portrayal of church and army is the *Carnival of the Ideologies* in which he satirized political demagoguery of the extreme right and extreme left. With a clever and imaginative jumbling of political symbols, he indicated their intentions to mislead and confuse.

On the center wall of the first landing of this staircase, he projected the brooding and idealistic face of the great patriot-priest *Hidalgo y Costilla* (fig. 96). In 1810 Hidalgo launched the Mexican revolt against Spain. The figure leans over the stairway in a punishing, almost apocalyptic manner. One hand is raised in an avenging gesture and the other waves a burning torch over the entire scene. He seems to stir into dynamic motion the figures who struggle below him.

Orozco carried out many other significant mural projects: the Supreme Court, the National School for Teachers, the National Museum of History, and others—each important in its own way. None of these, however, exceeds the power and impressiveness, the imaginative and emotional force of the murals in the Government Palace at Guadalajara. Here he joins the ranks of the greatest painters of our era.

IN this short history we have consciously limited ourselves to those we consider key figures in the development of Western painting. Many artists of undoubted importance have necessarily been given only passing mention and, in the same way, details in the lives and accomplishments of our fifty masters have been omitted.

For those interested in going beyond this survey we have provided a list of general books on the history of painting as well as individual studies devoted to most of the artists in this series.

The story just told is ended with the achievements of Orozco and six other leading modern artists. Here again these are not the only important painters of our century, but through them we have outlined most of the significant trends up to our own day and provided a background for the most recent developments.

Actually, the history of art, as of any human activity, never ends. At this very moment in the studios of New York, Rome, Paris, London and many other centers, young artists are at work whose names will someday be added to the list of great painters.

MORE BOOKS TO READ

IN GENERAL

Newton, Eric. *An Introduction to European Painting.* London: Longmans, Green, 1949.

Robb, David M. *The Harper History of Painting.* New York: Harper, 1951.

Berenson, Bernard. *The Italian Painters of the Renaissance.* London: Oxford University Press, 1932.

Mather, Frank J., Jr. *A History of Italian Painting.* New York: Holt, 1923.

McComb, Arthur K. *The Baroque Painters of Italy.* Cambridge: Harvard University Press, 1934.

Mather, Frank J., Jr. *Western European Painting of the Renaissance.* New York: Holt, 1939.

Fromentin, Eugene. *The Masters of the Past Time.* New York: Oxford University Press, 1948.

Puyvelde, Leo van. *The Flemish Primitives.* New York: Continental Book Center, 1948.

Dickinson, Helen A. *German Masters of Art.* New York: Stokes, 1924.

Myers, Bernard. *The German Expressionists.* New York: Praeger, 1957.

Wilenski, R. H. *An Introduction to Dutch Art.* London: Faber and Faber, 1937.

Hendy, Philip. *Spanish Painting.* London: Avalon, 1947.

Wilenski, R. H. *French Painting.* Boston: Branford, 1950.

Rocheblave, S. *French Painting in the XVIIIth Century.* New York: Hyperion, 1937.

Newton, Eric. *British Painting.* London: Longmans, Green, 1945.

Ritchie, Andrew C. *English Painters: Hogarth to Constable.* Baltimore: Johns Hopkins Press, 1942.

Barr, Alfred H. *What Is Modern Painting?* New York: Museum of Modern Art, 1949.

Cheney, Sheldon. *The Story of Modern Art*. New York: Viking, 1941.

Myers, Bernard S. *Modern Art in the Making*. New York: Whittlesey House, 1950.

Read, Herbert. *Art Now*. New York: Pitman, 1949.

Rewald, John. *The History of Impressionism*. New York: Museum of Modern Art, 1946.

Larkin, Oliver W. *Art and Life in America*. New York: Rinehart, 1949.

Myers, Bernard. *Mexican Painting in our Time*. New York: Oxford University Press, 1956.

INDIVIDUAL ARTISTS

BOTTICELLI—Yashiro, Yukio. *Sandro Botticelli and the Florentine Renaissance*. Boston: Hale, Cushman and Flint, 1929.

BRUEGHEL, PIETER, THE ELDER—Glück, Gustav. *Pieter Brueghel the Elder*. New York: Hyperion, 1937.

CARAVAGGIO—Hinks, Roger P. *Michelangelo Merisi da Caravaggio*. London: Faber, 1953.
Berenson, Bernard. *Caravaggio, His Incongruity and His Fame*. London: Faber, 1953.

CÉZANNE—Dorival, Bernard. *Cézanne*. New York: Continental Book Center, 1948.

CHAGALL—Sweeney, J. J. *Marc Chagall*. New York: Museum of Modern Art, 1948.

CHARDIN—Denvir, Bernard. *Chardin*. New York: Harper, 1950.

CONSTABLE—Clark, Kenneth. *Constable, the Hay Wain*. London: Humphries, 1946.

COPLEY—Flexner, James Thomas. *John Singleton Copley*. Boston: Houghton Mifflin, 1948.

COURBET—Zahar, Marcel. *Courbet*. New York: Harper, 1950.

DAUMIER—Lassaigne, Jacques. *Daumier*. London: Heinemann, 1938.

DAVID—Dowd, David L. *Pageant Master of the Republic*. Lincoln: University of Nebraska Press, 1949.

DEGAS—Manson, J. B. *The Life and Works of Edgar Degas*. London: Studio, 1927.

DELACROIX—Lassaigne, Jacques. *Delacroix*. New York: Harper, 1950.

DÜRER—Panofsky, Erwin. *Albrecht Dürer*. Princeton: Princeton University Press, 1948.

EYCK, JAN VAN—Baldass, Ludwig von. *Jan van Eyck*. New York: Phaidon, 1952.

GAINSBOROUGH—Millar, Oliver. *Gainsborough*. New York: Harper, 1949.

GAUGUIN—Rewald, John. *Gauguin*. New York: Oxford University Press, 1948.

GOGH, VINCENT VAN—Meier-Graefe, J. *Vincent van Gogh*. New York: Harcourt, Brace, 1933.

GOYA—Poore, Charles. *Goya*. New York: Scribner's, 1938.

Mayer, August L. *Francisco de Goya*. London: Dent, 1924.

GRECO, EL—Goldscheider, Ludwig. *El Greco*. London: Phaidon, 1949.

HOLBEIN—Ganz, Paul. *The Paintings of Hans Holbein*. New York: Phaidon, 1950.

Reinhardt, Hans. *Holbein*. New York: Hyperion, 1938.

HOMER—Goodrich, Lloyd. *Winslow Homer*. New York: Macmillan, 1944.

KANDINSKY—Rebay, Hilla von. *In Memory of Wassily Kandinsky*. New York: Solomon R. Guggenheim Foundation, 1945.

KOKOSCHKA—Hoffman, Edith. *Kokoschka, Life and Work*. London: Faber and Faber, 1946.

LEONARDO DA VINCI—Clark, Kenneth. *Leonardo da Vinci*. New York: Macmillan, 1939.

Valentin, Antonina. *Leonardo da Vinci*. New York: Viking, 1938.

MANET—Duret, Theodore. *Manet and the French Impressionists*. Philadelphia: Lippincott, 1910.

MATISSE—Fry, Roger. *Henri Matisse*. New York: Wehye, 1930.

Barr, Alfred H., Jr. *Matisse, His Art and His Public*. New York: Museum of Modern Art, 1951.

MICHELANGELO—de Tolnay, Charles. *Michelangelo*. Princeton: Princeton University Press, 1943, 1945.

Holroyd, Sir Charles. *Michelangelo Buonarroti*. New York: Scribner's, 1903.

OROZCO—Helm, MacKinley. *Man of Fire: José Clemente Orozco*. New York: Harcourt, Brace, 1953.

PICASSO—Barr, Alfred H., Jr. *Picasso: Fifty Years of His Art*. New York: Museum of Modern Art, 1946.

Cassou, Jean. *Picasso*. New York: Hyperion, 1940.

PIERO DELLA FRANCESCA—Longhi, Roberto. *Piero della Francesca*. New York: Oxford University Press, 1949.

POUSSIN—Sutro, Esther. *Nicolas Poussin*. Boston: Medici, 1923.

RAPHAEL—Suida, W. E. *Raphael*. London: Phaidon, 1948.

REMBRANDT—Rosenberg, Jakob. *Rembrandt*. 2 vols. Cambridge: Harvard University Press, 1948.

Borenius, Tancred. *Rembrandt, Selected Paintings*. New York: Oxford University Press, 1942.

RENOIR—Florisoone, Michel. *Renoir*. London: Heinemann, 1938.

RUBENS—Stevenson, R. A. M. *Rubens: Paintings and Drawings*. London: Phaidon, 1939.

TINTORETTO—Newton, Eric. *Tintoretto.* New York: Longmans, Green, 1950.

Tietze, Hans. *Tintoretto: Paintings and Drawings.* New York: Phaidon, 1948.

TITIAN—Gronau, Georg. *Titian.* New York: Scribner's, 1904.

Tietze, Hans. *Tiziano Vecelli; Paintings, Drawings.* New York: Phaidon, 1950.

TURNER—Mauclair, Camille. *Turner.* New York: Hyperion, 1939.

VELÁSQUEZ—Trapier, Elizabeth D. *Velásquez.* New York: The Hispanic Society of America, 1948.

VERMEER—Gowing, Lawrence. *Vermeer.* London: Faber, 1952.

Thienen, Frithjof van. *Vermeer.* New York: Harper, 1949.

A NOTE ON THE AUTHOR

Dr. Bernard Myers has won wide recognition for his works which range from college texts to scholarly studies and volumes like the *Encyclopedia of Painting*. Recently he supervised an extensive study of the creative artist in New York City which was undertaken on a grant from the Rockefeller Foundation. The results of this research are summarized in *Problems of the Younger American Artist*.

An inveterate traveler, Dr. Myers has spent much time in Latin America, particularly in Mexico, where he gathered material for his book on modern Mexican painting. On a grant from the Bolligen Foundation he spent two years in Germany studying the development of Expressionistic art.

At the present time Dr. Myers is lecturing at the City College of New York. He has also held teaching posts at Rutgers, New York University, the Art Students League, and the University of Texas where he was Guest Professor. As editor of art books for the McGraw-Hill Book Company, Dr. Myers goes to Europe once or twice a year in search of new titles for their publishing program as well as to advise on their *Encyclopedia of World Art*, a 15-volume project now being printed in Italy. His other writings include *Modern Art in the Making, Mexican Painting in our Time, The German Expressionists, Art and Civilization,* and *Understanding the Arts*.